Dealing
with
Loss
For Believers
&
Everyone

Eric Majors
www.EricMajors.com

Published by The Write For Right Project
www.WriteForRight.com

The Right For Right Project is an international, humanitarian
sustainable business project
of the publishing division of Xt Blue, Inc.
that is funded by a combination of donations, products sales and
the financial support of Xt Blue, Inc.
www.XtBlue.com
Please support the goals and work of the
Write For Right Project to help all artists in the world by buying
products sponsored by the Write For Right Project
and making donations to the Write For Right Project at
www.WriteForRight.com

DEDICATION

I dedicate this book to my mother who as taught me a great deal about loss during her struggle to deal with my brother's death.

I also dedicate to everyone in the world. We all have a critical role in assisting each other in overcoming loss. I share my experiences in the hope that other may benefit. My whish it to stimulate thinking, feeling and action that is constructive when experiencing all forms of loss and suffering.

CONTENTS

Acknowledgements

Acknowledgements

I acknowledge and praise God, our creator, from whom all good things flow and who allowed me to be alive, write this book and have all of the experiences of my life and to share life with others. I acknowledge and praise Jesus Christ for providing me with a role model that is loving, giving, caring and forgiving that accepts me with my faults and knows my true heart and intentions. Anything good that I have ever done and everything good that I do is only because of the patience, love, kindness and forgiveness that Jesus Christ continually asks from me. All that I have done wrong in my life is a result of my own human nature and selfishness that I strive to manage every day and for which I thank Jesus for his forgiveness that keeps me whole and new, as we are continually challenged to overcome our own selfishness and forgive the selfishness of others. Through continual seeking of the Holy Spirit with an ongoing study of and a relationship with Jesus Christ I do experience and understand true peace, love and fulfillment in all circumstances and I pray that it never ends and that everyone comes to know the presence of God and experience it every day.

I acknowledge and thank my wife Lisa, my son Ian, and my daughter Trinity, all of who insprite me to be a better man and teach me about love every day. I thank them for their patience and support while writing my books. I acknowledge and thank my mother, Marcy, for her unending generosity and my brother Jeff and his family who have all supported me when I needed it most. I would also like to thank my deceased brother, Steve, for the contributions he made in my life and although my father was absent for a great deal of my life I believe I learned valuable lessons from him and I do miss them both.

I acknowledge my dear friend and colleague, Derick Smith from South Africa, who has supported my family and myself and who took pains taking efforts to help me edit, implement and obtain a publisher for this book.

I acknowledge the great work of the Write For Right Project (WriteForRight.Com) and for selecting my works for publication. I encourage everyone who reads this book to please donate to Write For Right and purchase products produced by them so they can expand their great work to make the world a better place and to help people. Write For Right is creating opportunities for artists and writers like myself who have been released from prison to get jobs and have their works completed and published around the world as part of the "Write Now Project." Write For Right is helping people who are in prison and other disadvantaged groups of people all around the world to get the critical material and support needed for them to produce writings and works of art that improve the health and lives of everyone concerned and bring important messages to the people of the world.

I acknowledge all of my friends and associates who have supported me, forgiven me and given me a second chance in life and who appreciate my intentions.

I would also like to acknowledge all of the people and prison staff that I met while I was incarcerated at various institutions that were supportive of myself and others. In particular I would like to thank all of the inmates, staff and volunteers who were supportive of my family and I in the FPC Pensacola, the Denver County Jail, the Tallahassee DTC, the Oklahoma DTC and the U.S. Marshals Service who did show a great deal of care and compassion for me and my case while I was under their supervision. There are a number of caring and compassionate prison staff members without which the experience of prison would be completely inhumane and even more counterproductive than it usually is.

I have not forgotten the inmates and the FPC 5pm prayer group sessions. I will keep you all in my prayers and pray for your earliest release and health and welfare of all parties. I will always cherish the conversations and friendships that I had with the Chaplin, Richard, Dean, Laz, Peter, Maurice, Kevin, Toepfer, Scott, Rusty, Jimmy and so many other good people that I could fill the pages of this book if I listed them all.

One thing that I can acknowledge is that there are a lot of good people in the United States who are spending very long terms of incarceration in prison who never should have been sentenced to prison in the first place. But that is a topic for another book that God willing, I will also have published.

In addition, there are special people that were so supportive of my family and myself that thanking them seems hardly enough. When I was in the prison camp they helped us in so many ways. Let me thank you, my friends: Tory Lynette and his parents, Skip and Barbra, Paul Stabnow, Jeff Guzy and Paul Richter. And I apologize for omitting othes herein that helped my wife. Words cannot describe how much your support meant to us at a time when I wasn't able to provide all of the support to my family that I really wanted to be able to provide.

Introduction

This book is written from my own prospective as a Christian; however, I have written the book in such a manner that the ideas and methods within can be used by people of almost every faith and even by those who do not believe in God. As a Christian I feel that it is important to understand that the personal application of the methods within this book are not for the attainment of heaven or forgiveness of God, but a way of becoming what we are created for and minimizing suffering. According to my own belief as a Christian there is nothing we can do to gain entry to heaven other than to choose to believe in, and accept the grace and forgiveness granted to us by God. This is the very grace that was demonstrated by the life of Jesus, who even forgave his persecutors whilst he was dying on the cross.

There is a profound message and comfort in this forgiveness. Many believers can acknowledge that God forgives them, but this is of limited use if the believer does not also forgive themselves. I could go on and on about the importance of forgiveness, and, God willing, I will most likely do so in subsequent books.

Why does God forgive us? He loves us; certainly not because of our thoughts or actions. We are not perfect, even by our own standards, but then again, maybe we are perfect in that we were designed to live a life that includes mistakes, failures and pain, as well as achievements, successes and joy. Therein we are perfect by design as we are fulfilling our intended purpose.

We grapple with sin, all of which is derived from selfishness. I have come to realize that sin and selfishness are the very same thing, and that if I replace the word sin with selfishness many of the mysteries are clarified. I consider my every day an ongoing mission in life is to overcome selfishness in every way that it manifests itself in me.

Some people say that the road to hell is paved with good intentions. I disagree. I have come to believe that our intentions are fundamental. No one can guarantee success or perfection when they set out to do so, because of all of the unknown events that can occur while we try to do something. But having good intentions is important because we know (and God knows) our hearts, regardless of how well we perform, and regardless of our success or failure. Even when our intentions are bad we are still be forgiven by God if we are able to acknowledge our transgressions and simply ask to be forgiven. We can also forgive ourselves, and this is important. Forgiveness is a decision and we don't need a reason to forgive anyone, including ourselves.

Our not knowing the future, not knowing the details of the past, our perceived trials and failures, the experience of both good and bad; for me this is part of the perfect human experience. How can we not be perfect if we were designed to experience both success and failure, both pain and joy? For these reasons I believe that we are all perfect in the eyes of God, and I take comfort in every experience that I have, good and bad, and yield to the universe and to God with peace.

Chapter 1: The Conditioned Experience of Loss

The entire subject of dealing with loss could really be entitled, "dealing with the condition of loss" because, in reality, we never really gain or lose anything. We are merely guests in the universe while we are alive, and, when we pass away, the most we can hope to take with us are the memories of our relationships and events in our lives. Every loss or gain is only a matter of perception because we adopt the false idea that there are objects to be gained or lost in the first place. In order to lose something you must first have it. Therefore, when we look back on our perceived loss, there must actually be a net gain because we were fortunate to have experienced whatever we had, for however long we had it, or there would not be any problems letting go. Yet in most cases human nature causes us to focus on the sorrow of the loss rather than being grateful for what we experienced. We don't own anything. We have relationships and experiences.

As part of our conditioned nature we often look at our past experiences as some distant event (or place) that gets further and further away from us as time goes by. As our past "slips away" we tend to see our happy experiences and loved ones left behind us, as though they were left on islands that we are flying away from while returning home after a vacation. To make matters worse, instead of seeing our daily life to which we return as a gift, we perceive it as a lonely, isolated, routine, ordinary, uninteresting and uneventful place to which we have somehow become enslaved.

Chapter 2: The Nature of Sentimental Attachments

When I was in prison, I was lucky enough to spend most of my time at a prison camp where I could have weekend visitations with my wife and two children in a pleasant visitation area that resembled a large back yard. We were very appreciative and grateful because this type of visitation facility does not exist in most U.S. prisons. In most U.S. prisons the entire process of visitation is something that represents a cost to the prison system in time, human resources, and money, and thus visitations in all forms are slowly being restricted or essentially eliminated in U.S. prisons and state and county jails with little or no regard for the debilitating effects this has on inmates, their families and society. Most U.S. jails and prisons claim that they allow and even encourage visitations, but further investigation reveals that the processes and practices of visitation in the majority are essentially discouraging, inhumane and inadequate to yield any beneficial effects. The system does not help prisoners, their families or their communities strengthen or retain ties.

In some prison facilities where I stayed there were no visitations permitted at all. I represented myself as my own attorney in the Federal District Court and as such I was required to make personal appearance in court for some communications. Today there are reliable and inexpensive video conferencing technologies that allow people to make appearances in courts from remote locations using video conferencing. These video conferencing systems are successfully being used in many developed nations around the world, but the United States has yet to implement this cost effective technology throughout the federal prison system, and still relies on a very costly and punitive method to physically transport prisoners to and from courts. Thus, when I won an appeal in my case I was transported to and from Pensacola Prison Camp in Florida and the Federal District Court in Denver Colorado, which had jurisdiction in my case.

My family had moved from Boca Raton, Florida to Pensacola Florida near the prison camp in order to be able visit with me as much as possible, but when I needed to appear in person in the Federal District Court of Colorado I was not able to obtain a furlough to go back and forth to the court at my own expense and thus I was not able to see my family while I was dealing with my legal case. The process of my transfers between Florida and Colorado lasted for several weeks during which I spent my time traveling and residing at various county jails and Federal Prisons throughout the United

States.

This process of transportation is considered by inmates to be an additional form of punishment in itself. They refer to these lengthy, loathsome and unpredictable transports between prisons as "diesel therapy," and from my experience the entire process was at times dangerous, exhausting and demoralizing. The prison transportation system made it very difficult for me to act as my own attorney and for me to adequately defend myself, which resulted in a lot of confusion in my case and in me being unable to effectively express myself to the court. I later learned that in many cases the U.S. Department of Justice often intentionally uses "diesel therapy" as a means to wear down certain prisoners and to keep them from being able to adequately defend themselves. The worst part for me was knowing that there was no way for me to visit with or see my family throughout the duration of the entire ordeal, which lasted over 7 months. At one large county jail where I spent over 5 months there was no visitation allowed at all (I do not consider 60 minutes per week of video conferencing that is allowed as a visitation). Virtually all other civilized countries in the world handle the issue of visitation with much more respect and in much more humanitarian ways than prisons in the United States do, but this is a subject for another book.

Fortunately for my family and me I was in the minimum security Pensacola Federal Prison Camp where I spent most of the time of my sentence. There was grass, a pavilion, tables to sit at, a basketball hoop and even some balls to play with. Face to face visitations were allowed from 5pm-to 8:30pm on Friday nights and from 8am to 3pm on Saturdays, Sundays and some holidays unless there was some kind of power failure. This liberal schedule was astonishing compared to most prisons. When the visitations were over, and the families had left, I was allowed to walk around and sit in the area where we had just had our visit. I would become sentimental about all of the items that we used. If I saw a stone that my daughter or son had played with I might take it and put it in my pocket. I would think about them having touched the objects and so part of them was on the stone.

I would look for their footprints in the sand and remains of the games that we played. I felt sorrowful about the fact that they were no longer there and about having to wait an entire week to see them again.

Chapter 3: Overcoming Attachment

Eventually, while meditating on the issue, I realized that I did not need to revisit these areas and that the rocks that they had touched actually had no real significance at all other than what I was assigning to them. I realized that the feelings that I had about these objects were not coming from the objects themselves but instead they originated inside me. I realized that my family was not out there and I "in here" but that actually we were together in spirit all of the time. We were connected all of the time, no matter where we were, because of the experiences that we shared and not because of the items that we shared together. The items were only special while we were using them together, because we were using them. When we were done with them they were no more special than any other rocks, footprints or sticks. I must also state that I believe all rocks, dirt and sticks are gifts from God but I don't need to carry them all around either.

Similarly, my daughter would frequently mention how much she wanted to return to our old house where we had lived before I had checked into prison. I missed that house too. We had so many great memories there. But then I realized that just like the stones, footprints and sticks in the prison yard, it was not the house that was special at all. It was only special while we lived in it because of our presence in it. When we left it became simply a house again with nothing any more special about it than any other house.

Chapter 4: Shifting from Suffering and Pain to Joy and Peace

At all times WE were the source of the love, joy and peace that we bestowed upon the house and it was not the house that imparted these qualities to us. We could access joy, peace and love at any time that we desired to do so even while we were experiencing great adversity and suffering in life.

The deciding factor in accessing joy, peace or overcoming loss is to exchange our default way of thinking about loss that requires us to cling to memories, property and people instead of realizing that TIME IS NOT a stream that carries experiences further and further from us, but rather TIME IS a stream of experiences that flows into us. It fills up our memory as we ingest it and it nourishes us like a stream of pure water. Like some molecules of water become part of us and some passes through us, this stream cleans out our system and removes impurities from our consciousness, transforming us forever (for the better if we allow it). Like water that nourishes us, we have access to the good memories and feelings at any time we choose, and we can choose to discard the waste of undesirable experiences in order for us to learn, transform and evolve.

Chapter 5: Experiences and Memories Add To Our Lives

The experiences and the associated items that were

involved in the experiences are never lost. They help to build us and they are integrated into us starting from the instant that we experience them until we die. I came to realize that wherever I am, no matter where I go, for all time, I carry the experiences that I had with my family, the feelings of love, peace and contentment that we shared, in the visitation area and in our previous homes. I don't need to live in the house again or to ever see it again for the experiences to be integrated into my being. I don't need to carry sticks, stones or other items with me in order for the experiences shared with them to accompany me. All my past experiences are integrated into my very being. The experience is with me wherever or whenever I AM, not where these external items are. From this perspective the items are not external at all; they are already part of me, connected to me no matter where I go in the universe. I don't need to keep a stockpile and storehouse of material artifacts from my life in order to save or recall the essence of the experiences that are already part of my being.

Chapter 6: Unhealthy Attachments to Memories and Ideas

In addition to becoming attached to things, it is also default human nature to become sentimental about thoughts, ideas and memories. While it is fantastic to be able to recall past events and memories and relive them in our minds as much as we like, this practice can also become an unnecessary encumbrance. Reliving old memories can become a time consuming ritual that prevents us from having new experiences in life if we are not careful. If we are not mindful of what we are doing we might become sentimental about revisiting past memories so often that we feel guilty if we fail to engage in a daily ritual of reliving the same past memories again and again. This guilt may arise particularly in cases where our loved ones are no longer physically present with us due to death, physical distance or for whatever reason. We may be tempted to feel that we are being disrespectful of our loved ones if we don't go through lengthy remembrances of them every single day. Again, the cure to this way of thinking is to simply recognize that, when we become dependent on reliving the memories, it prohibits us from actively engaging in the present day and building new experiences as life and God intend for us to have. It is important to avoid becoming stuck.

Chapter 7: Healthy Integration of Memories and Ideas

Consider this example. If I peel a grapefruit and eat it for breakfast today, and it tastes particularly wonderful to me, then I might remember that grapefruit the next day or at some future meal. I may recount to friends how sweet the grapefruit was that I once had. I am grateful for the grapefruit when I am eating it and I thank God for providing it to me, but I don't re-live the experience of eating the grapefruit every day to express gratitude. I don't have to. Once I have eaten the grapefruit it becomes part of my body. It nourishes my body now and forever. The experience of the grapefruit itself is therefore integrated into me forever. The grapefruit and its experience is part of me. I no longer need to revisit the memory of the grapefruit in order to derive its benefits. I have it forever, wherever I go until I die. Even after death we can appreciate the positive impact it had on me while I was alive, without having to be in remembrance of it. The grapefruit is part of everything I do once I experience it because it becomes integrated into me just like all of the other experiences that I have in my life.

Chapter 8: Mourning as a Healthy Tool

Am I suggesting in this book that mourning the loss of a loved one is unnecessary? For some it may be unnecessary and for others it may indeed be necessary. It is perfectly natural for us to feel sorrow that we may not be able to visit a person tomorrow because of some type of real physical or other separation. Some people are under the impression that they are alone when they suffer and that they must either hide their suffering or try to re-invent the wheel by coming up with their own methods of dealing with pain by themselves.

The truth is that we, the contemporary people of this day and age are not the only people in the world who have struggled with the pain of sorrow from both real and imagined loss. The concepts and processes of mourning are a natural part of human existence that have been contemplated, experienced, explored, developed and used throughout world and recorded history. Fortunately, we have a vast database of recorded experiences, traditions and methods that have been successfully used by people for centuries to help overcome the negative effects of the experience of loss.

Based on my experience the most revolutionary, effective state of the art methods offered by our modern science of medicine and psychology and self help teachers for overcoming the emotional pain and suffering from the experience of loss are all essentially re-worked and re-discovered versions of the same fundamental processes that have already been discovered and successfully used throughout history as expressed and recorded in historical, scientific, spiritual and religious texts. In this book I will simply summarize and offering yet another description of these very same popular processes that have been proven to be most effective in overcoming the undesirable effects that result for most people from their experience of loss.

Chapter 9: Unhealthy Emotional Practices & Reactions to Loss

Contrary to the popular modern beliefs of many people being overly stoic or attempting to control the strong emotional energies associated with anger and sorrow by intentionally suppressing them, ignoring them or postponing their experience through use of excessive drugs and alcohol is a dangerous and counterproductive approach to the problem. Attempting to suppress any emotional energy including laughter can cause physical discomfort and disease ("dis-ease"). Mental instability and may also result in direct emotional and physical harm to the practitioners and their loved ones.

Chapter 10: Suppression and the Blame Game

Telling yourself or others to "not express" their pain or that any of the emotions that come upon them are wrong is as silly as telling someone not to laugh when something genuinely humorous occurs. One thing that is certain is that every person in the world will experience some form of emotion in their lives and that the energy that accompanies some emotions can at times appear to be overwhelming.

Another certainty is that people are not the creators of their own thoughts and emotions. Thoughts and emotions simply arise in human beings from time to time without anyone being able to tell why they come in every case. It is true that we do have a choice as to what we decide to think about but most have not developed the complete control of mind to prevent random thoughts and feelings from presenting. Thus, in most cases we are not the exclusive creators of our own thoughts.

If people where able to be the exclusive creators of their own thoughts and emotions then there would be far fewer problems between people in the world because they could consciously choose only optimal thoughts and emotions to arise at just the right times. But this is not the case in reality, as we often witness others and experience with ourselves. There are situations where we know what will lead to constructive outcomes but we fail to take constructive right action because we allow ourselves to be lead by our emotional energy rather than learning how to harness and direct our emotional energy in positive ways.

Learning how to deal with our emotional energy is one of the first charges that God makes to Cain in the Bible in Genesis 4.6-7, "Then the Lord said to Cain, "Why are you angry? Why is your face downcast? If you do what is right, will you not be accepted? But if you do not do what is right, sin [SELFISHNESS] is crouching at your door; it desires to have you, but you must rule over it."

Similarly in the book of James 3.2 James says, "For all of us make many mistakes. If someone does not make any mistakes when he speaks, he is perfect and able to control his whole body." What is it that keeps us from controlling our speaking and acting in alignment with the advice given by God in the Bible? It is our own selfishness and lack of ability to control the onset of our own emotional energy that causes us to falter. It is our own impatience, our own desire to be "right" and to be the winner of all arguments that blinds us from the truth that actually we can be certain of nothing and we must acknowledge and respect others and their opinions and act with humility and continual self analysis if we are to live in peace. I agree with Mark Twain when he said, "It ain't what you don't know that gets you into trouble. It's what you know for sure that just ain't so."

Christ puts it into very simple terms, "If any of you wants to be my follower, you must turn from your selfish ways, take up your cross daily, and follow me." I have come to realize that overcoming selfishness in my own life is the single most important mission in my life. I have found that my best approach to dealing with my own selfishness is to live a lifestyle of continual self awareness and practice of self observation. I must continually monitor myself, correcting and adjusting my courses of action and thought, to be in alignment with my best estimates of what Christ would like for me to do. And even my own estimation of what Christ is requiring from me evolves and changes over time, just as the meanings of the passages of the Bible and other religious texts that I study. Even advise that I receive from my spiritual mentors, family and friends can have new meaning as I evolve and circumstances change.

Using my approach I must also acknowledge that I am not perfect and that I will make mistakes, and, in order for me to evolve, I must forgive myself of these mistakes as and when I realize them. Imperfection and unforeseen circumstances are part of the optimal experience of human life. Thus, I take comfort in knowing that the perfect human experience involves imperfection, and that I should not allow myself to get caught up in the act of self condemnation for too long or I will be unable to move on with my life, grow and learn from my mistakes. This forgiveness goes for other people too. I have to be able to let others move on with their lives, grow and evolve. I must be able to forgive them for the mistakes that they make, even if they don't know they've made them. Some of Christ's last words were "forgive them for they know not what they do…"

Many people condemn themselves and others, placing blame on them for having or causing certain undesirable feelings. They waste precious time trying to figure out why these feelings come.   An important issue is how a person behaves in light of any thoughts and feelings that they do experience for any reason. There is no point in blaming yourself or anyone else for the emotions that they experience. There is nothing to be gained by telling others that there is something wrong with them for experiencing the emotions that they experience because what we are most concerned about is not the feelings and emotional energy that arise, but how best to harness that energy and use it for constructive purposes.

All emotional energy is a gift from God, even undesirable emotional energy that we refer to as pain, anger and fear. It is up to each one of us to learn how to use and direct the flow of all emotional energy into constructive action. It is up to each of us to also consciously choose to shift from negative thinking and action to positive thinking and action.

Consciously choosing to redirect the emotional energy that we feel or to harness this energy for positive expression or use is not the same thing as controlling your emotions by suppressing them. There is healthy control and expression that leads to positive action and unhealthy control which usually involves suppression of emotions or acting out in destructive and negative ways.

In order for us to consciously choose to harness all of

our emotional energy and redirect it for constructive purposes it is not necessary for us to spend time trying to figure out why these undesirable emotions occur. It is far more important to practice and become good at using all emotional energy for positive results. When a person gets good at managing their emotional energy in a way that leads to positive changes in action and behavior, then the answer to the question of why the person was having undesirable emotions in the first place typically reveals itself without any effort. The answers to the question "why" typically become available, without any effort, by those people who successfully learn how to change their own behavior through the process of conscious emotional energy management.

Telling yourself that you must suppress your own emotions and emotional energies in order to assist others in their process of dealing with loss is not a good choice. A better choice is to allow yourself to acknowledge and experience your sorrow and anger and to express it to others in a constructive ways. The better choice is always to practice consciously channeling undesirable emotional energy into something positive. Expressing and describing to other people, in a kind and caring and sincere way, the feelings that you are experiencing can be enough in most cases to help the undesirable emotional energy to be relieved in a healthy way. It is not necessary to reveal every detail of your emotional state to others that may cause conflict, but self expression is an art form that must be developed in order to have as peaceful and joyful life as possible.

It is imperative that people find healthy ways to express what they are going through and channel any undesirable emotional energy into constructive action as and whenever they occur.

Chapter 11: A Traditional Healthy Mourning Process

I think that just as the ancient people recognized, setting aside a period of mourning is a good and healthy practice. One should allow for ample time to indulge completely n the experience of sorrow rather than attempting to be 'stoic' and pretending to be aloof, or to avoiding the feelings of sorrow by intentional suppression or use of alcohol or drugs. In order to ever complete the process of sorrow, one must go through the sorrow and allow it to diminish and exhaust itself over time.

How long should one allow? Some cultures set a time limit on mourning of 2 weeks and others 2 months. There is no optimal length of time that I am aware of but the important thing is to define a space and time during which mourning takes place and then they move on with life without being encumbered by the process of mourning. The mourning process should be a tool that liberates you not a process that keeps you stuck in sorrow, unable to evolve.

For some people mourning may go on for years before it is diminished to unnoticeable levels. The important thing is that we continue to move away from debilitating sorrow and back into engagement with life in the present. In order to do this we must make a conscious decision to seek a way of being that is unencumbered by the sentimental handicap of our attachment to reliving the experience of loss.

Most people would agree that our loved ones who are not physically present with us would most likely want for us NOT BE permanently oppressed by our attachment to mourning our perceived loss. Like the grapefruit, we have the opportunity let go of the physical presence of the loved one, replace it with joy and be appreciative of the experiences that we had, which we have ingested into our being, and that have nourished us and are part of us just like the grapefruit.

Chapter 12: Oppression and Forgiveness

Yet another, more sinister way that we can become locked into an endless cycle of self oppression, depression and perpetual mourning, is failure to accept the fact that we are not perfect, and hence forgive ourselves. By failing to forgive ourselves, or failing to accept God's plans for the universe, our psyche automatically uses our own guilt to do the work of Lucifer by oppressing us. I call this scenario automatic self oppression.

Let me give you some examples. In December 2012, a horrific event occurred that no rational person would ever wish to happen. Several people, the majority being small kindergarten children, were murdered by a disturbed gunman who took his own life. Our first reaction is guilt, blaming ourselves for not being able to prevent the event from occurring. Our second reaction is blaming God and asking why God allowed this to happen.

In the first case we oppress ourselves because we have bought into the idea that we are not truly mourning if we don't punish ourselves for not being able to prevent an event that we never intended in the first place. As a result we do Lucifer's work for him by using up our God given energy and power to oppress ourselves indefinitely without Lucifer having to lift a finger. Thus Lucifer laughs at us and his victory. The cure to this affliction of guilt is twofold: first realize that no matter how much we plan for the best, the universe can still deliver chaos and suffering as part of life that cannot be foreseen; second, we must exercise liberal forgiveness for ourselves just as

Christ taught us to do. Christ demonstrated the extent to which we should forgive people when he forgave, with his last breath, the very people who crucified him. Our ability to forgive ourselves and others will help end the first cycle of self oppression. We live in a culture where we are encouraged to believe that closure comes to victims when offenders are punished. This is a falsehood that is dangerous to believe.

Chapter 13: Why does God allow bad things to happen?

The next practice that will lead to self oppression is engaging in thinking that creates distance between us and God. We often seek to justify our undesirable emotions and negative resulting behavior in relation to our anger at God for things not working out as we had wanted. In dealing with genuine loss a more subtle discontent arises from the inevitable negative feelings brought by the question, "Why does God allow this suffering to take place?"

The Bible explains the answer to that question in many ways. In the book of Job, and in other places throughout the Bible, it is made clear to us that God's ways are not ours and that we should not dwell on our inability to answer the question about why such negative events are allowed to occur. We must become comfortable and exercise faith in God that "all things work for the greatness of God," even the negative things that we may not understand.

A more important resolution to this question is also answered in the New Testament, when the apostles asked Christ about a blind man that Christ cured. The apostles asked why the man was blind in the first place. They asked if it had to do with the sins of the man or the sins of the man's parents. Jesus replied that the man was blind so that the Glory of God could be shown on earth when Jesus cured him.

Consider this further. God could easily smite Lucifer whenever he wants to, as evidenced in the book of Job wherein Lucifer could not even afflict Job until God gave Lucifer permission. So there is some reason why God allows Lucifer to exist and perform his works. While I don't claim to know the exact details, consider the possibility that one reason God allows Lucifer to continue to exist is so that man can experience the Glory of God and the pleasure and joy that contrasts with the experience of pain and suffering. The experience of pain and suffering, when endured, leads to a transformation of our being into a closer more blissful connection with God. Without pain, suffering and anguish we may have no reason to ever build our relationship with God and have the great joy that is derived through enduring hard trials and seeking communion with God.

It is God who is the provider of all peace, joy and fulfillment! The name Lucifer means, "the bringer of light," so wherever evil is made, good is also made. If we have nothing that we consider evil, then we have no contrasting thing to define good by. There is a balance in the universe and wherever Lucifer creates problems the light of God will follow, and bring a hundredfold joy and restitution at a time appointed by God. If the experience of joy were not hundredfold more intense than suffering then it would not be ecstasy.

Chapter 14: Do you really practice faith?

Therefore, when considering the plight of the kindergarten children that were gunned to death in their classrooms, also consider that we may suffer more the harder we try to understand "why." This is because understanding the specifics surrounding the shooting may be like trying to understand the reasons why any other natural disasters occur. It is simply not intended or necessary for us to understand the answer to the question why but rather to have faith that all things occur for good according to the plans of God.

Of course we have an investigation by the authorities of the details surrounding negative events in order to correct those responsible and to help prevent future undesirable events from occurring, but this is not the investigation that I am referring to. The fruitless investigation that only leads to suffering that I am referring to is the one that diverts us from realizing higher levels of awareness of truth in the moment, and instead leads us into false spiritual, mystical or celestial reasoning rather than the positive potentials that can be extrapolated from these events.

When we investigate for the purposes of practicing our Christianity or our higher spiritual enlightenment then we investigate "what is" in relation to our faith in God rather than our doubt in God. It is essential that we do not rely exclusively on what we initially perceive in events as part of our basic nature. Indeed, the Bible encourages us to "Seek and you shall find." If we seek darkness and uncertainty then we will find that. If we choose to seek out the excellence of God then we will bask in the love of God as we are directed to do as Christians.

Chapter 15: How do we know what is the right time?

For example, when we seek to find what is truly important in relation to events, we do not concern ourselves with aspects that we do not have any certainty about, but we rely instead on objective facts. In the example of the school shooting we might first consider the children that are dead. If you believe in God then the children are with God and what could be better than that? If you do not believe in God then the children are not able to think or care about what happened and so they are at peace. Either case should make us happy. Just because we have an idea that their life was cut short, we also have no proof that their life did not end at the most optimal time. For this reason it might even be disrespectful to their memory and to God for us to assume that we know best what the length and composition of their lives should have been.

Chapter 16: Survivors and the Glory of God

Of course, as I already stated, the parents of the deceased children have every right to, and should engage in whatever mourning that their experience of sorrow dictates they should endure. And we should help them to get through their mourning, no matter how long it takes. We must continue to support them until the memory of the blessing of the experience of their children that is now integrated into their being is considered by those parents to be a net positive gain rather than a loss.

Similarly, the children who survived this terrible nightmare will undoubtedly have obstacles to overcome in their lives and memories that will need to be reconciled. However, before we are tempted to cling to the idea with 100% certainty that this terrible event will forever ruin the lives of the children who survived, and all of the effected parents, we must consider the profound possibilities of how this event may yet reveal the Glory of God.

We have indeed been visited by Lucifer who has caused darkness to occur. Yet this too will bring the light of God that brings joy, peace and love a hundred times greater than the suffering. We must face the fact that while one man, used by Lucifer, killed children and others, now the survivors are undoubtedly being offered overwhelming, loving kindness from people all over the planet, including renowned and celebrated experts who are ready to provide spiritual, psychological, humanitarian, educational and financial support to the survivors, the likes of which they would have never had access to before.

As a result these children and parents lives will be touched with an ultimate good. They will be touched in a way that can not only cure these people of suffering, but may also enable these children to become well adjusted in spite of their experience. The net positive results may enable the children who survived to become even better contributors to the human race than they ever might have been if this event never took place. In this way what Lucifer intended now becomes a display of love, the

Glorious God and how evil can be overpowered by the light that follows it.

Chapter 17: We don't know what we don't know

I would like to share with you other possibilities for us to consider regarding the experience of those children who were killed. These possibilities are illustrated by a story that shows how limited our own understanding is of tragic events in general, and their purpose and meaning in our lives.

In this true story a young child survives the killing of his parents in their own house by criminals. When the child was confronted by the police to ask about the details of the death of his parents the child said that after awakening from loud noises a man entered his room and told him that his parents were going away and not to worry because they would be OK. The man sat with the child for some time and held him. The police showed mug shots to the child to see if he could identify who the man in his room might have been because they suspected that the man was part of the criminal party that entered the house. After exhausting all of the mug shots, the child pointed to a picture of the face of a man that was behind the desk of the detectives and said, "That is the man that I saw that stayed with me." The picture was a picture of Jesus Christ.

These events speak of the very real possibility that the children who were being shot may have also been spared from the total experience of their own death because Christ may have been with them at that time.

Chapter 18: The illusion of control and the pain it causes

We are conditioned into believing that we alone are the masters of our destinies, and thus we feel pain when things don't go our way.   We live in a culture that advertises and sells many products including religious and spiritual works that reinforce the idea that you can do and be anything you choose and that you deserve the best and only good things.   Thus there are a lot of high expectations being promoted to us without any clear pathway to obtain these "gifts" that we deserve, and without any qualification about what is actually best for you.

The biggest danger in leaving people with the impression that they deserve to get whatever their hearts desire is in leaving it up to people to decide what is actually best for themselves. What feels good to us, is not necessarily good for us. Eating ice-cream feels great on the tongue of most people, but eating it for breakfast lunch and dinner will lead to an accelerated death.   Unfortunately, many people were not brought up in an environment that has taught them about the attitudes and behaviors that will genuinely lead to health and happiness.

Thus, telling someone that they deserve all good things, without providing any specific targets against which to measure their own success and what is good, is dangerous. Without any role models or values to live by, it is very likely that many people may actually engage in meditations that lead to behaviors that are selfish, unhealthy and counterproductive to achieving any happiness at all. I've seen some people meditate themselves into pure arrogance because they were not guided or restrained in their own practices by any spiritual framework such as Christianity, Buddhism or Zen. I agree that people are deserving of good things and that they can manifest good for themselves, provided that they meditate on what is actually good for themselves rather than mere corporal desires and lusts that lead to selfishness, arrogance, dangerous liaisons and disease.

I enjoy and practice both prayer and eastern meditation in order to help guide my intention and purpose, as well as my thinking and feeling. I have learned that without fixing my goals by modeling myself after a specific role model such as Christ, then all I am doing is praying for, meditating and indulging myself in my own selfish desires that can lead to very unhealthy, damaging behavior that affects myself, my loved ones and my relationships. I have also learned to temper my expectations in life with the reality that I am in a state of co-creation and I am not the only influencing power in the universe.

Yes, it is true that you have a great deal of power and control over what actions you take in relation to your life and circumstances. You have a great deal of power to learn how to guide yourself in your experience of life in order to try to achieve goals. However, what most often leads to failure in the practice of "you can do it all" is the fact that you are only the co-creator of your life. In addition to your own desires and will and efforts, which may appear to be under your control, there are many more people, objects, events and circumstances, that are entirely out of your control, that may also have a direct influence on your actual results and perceived successes and failures.

Throughout my life as a coach I have observed and experienced myself the great suffering that people can inflict on themselves when they worry intently over things which they believe they control. The more that I observe what is really under our control compared to what we think is under our control, the more I conclude that our perception of control consists mostly of assumptions and illusions that we make up in our own minds. As humans it is in our nature to believe that we have control over everything when in fact we have control over very little, if anything. If we work to develop our own abilities to master our default thinking and feeling, then we might have some control over the planning of our future and how we react to circumstances, thoughts and emotions as they arise. Sadly many people don't even have enough effective control over themselves in response to their own emotional energies and unhealthy thinking to keep them from engaging in bad behavior.

In the new testament of the Bible Christians are taught to use the words hope and faith. Hope is a word that acknowledges the possibility of failure and understands that success may not always occur because of the co-creation process. Similarly the word faith is literally a choice to believe and act on something that "cannot be seen or proven." In contrast, words or phrases that we use in relation to present and future outcomes that can lead to unrealistic expectations, and delusions of include "have to", "need to" and "must."

By choosing to have hope and faith that all things will be for the greater good we can live more comfortable lives that those people who become enraged over their perceived failures. We hope and therefore take a course of action, and if failure does occur it does not cripple us because we have faith. We do not punish ourselves or others for failing, but we take as best corrective action as we can, forgive ourselves and others and move on as fully accountable people who are willing to make restitution. For those who exercise faith, failures are learning experiences, from which we evolve and can either try again or choose a new course of action altogether, or choose no further action at all.

Chapter 19: Having faith by surrendering uncertainty to God

A certain, overwhelming comfort and peace is available to everyone at any time, no matter what the circumstances, in the practice of surrendering. When we consciously choose to surrender all present and future events to God, even if it means that we may suffer and die, we are able to rest and experience true peace.

When circumstances are truly out of our control some pray to God to ask what they should do and this is always a good idea. However I believe there are certain circumstances that require us to do nothing other than pray to God to handle the situation on our behalf. The praying itself is all that can be done when nothing else you are trying is working. This is particularly true when we are dealing with loved ones who appear to be unresponsive to our attempts to help them and even in cases where children appear to ignore our authority. It is also true when we feel we are losing control over our own temptations and selfishness. In these cases the best prayer is to acknowledge that we are not in control of everything and to simply ask God, "God, this is out of my control, will you please take this over for me? Please take this feeling from me, I give it to you to handle because I do not know what to do with it myself and it is overwhelming." In the case of dealing with loved ones we don't give up trying but we simply change our position from forcing something to occur to allowing whatever must occur and simply standing by when help is eventually needed. We don't give up trying, but we relieve ourselves of the feeling of burden that is associated with something that we feel is our responsibility but is actually out of our control.

There is a great sence of peace that becomes available when we simply acknowledge that not everything is under our control and all our responsibility alone.

If we believe in God we can have faith that, whatever happens that appears to conflict with our own prayers, was meant to happen as part of the purpose and experience set of our lives. We remain thankful for our entire experience and gift of being alive no matter what the circumstances. If we practice faith then we have faith in all possibilities of good, and we alter our daily direction in order to help manifest those good realities as best that we can.

One of the greatest tools that we have available to us in order to overcome our perceived loss is to practice our faith. We Christians often chastise ourselves unnecessarily for not having faith. However, we fail to realize that it is wrong for us to be angry at ourselves, or others, for not having faith, because faith is not necessarily something that comes naturally but rather it is a method of dealing with life that only comes through practice. Thich Nhat Hanh is a great Vietnamese peace activist and theologian who practices Buddhism and Christianity. In his book "Living Buddha Living Christ" Thich Nhat Hanh explains that simply claiming to be a Christian and uttering the words and prayers of any faith and going to church does not make any person an effective Christian. What is necessary, in order to experience the benefits of our faith, is to actively engage in the personal and collective study of the subject of our spirituality, every day, using the Bible and as many other books as we can find. This is in order to become good practitioners of our faith. We need to study our faith just as we would study to become doctors. I have only been actively studying with a high level of intensity since I was 37 years old. I have discovered that even if I had 5 lifetimes I would not be able to read all of the spiritual philosophy books and watch all of the videos that can help improve my own spiritual walk.

As I re-read the Bible, often the scriptures take on new meaning as I grow in experience and new understanding. Practicing faith has the effect of replacing loss and sorrow with joy and relief.

Chapter 20: The practice of Faith by changing our thinking

So how do we practice faith in order to turn sorrow into joy? Sorrow is our normal, initial, default human reaction to any undesirable event because sorrow takes the least mental and physical energy to manifest. Getting out of sorrow requires work in the form of thinking. The apostle Paul states that when we are living in the Spirit it is our mind that is changed. Changing our mind requires some work. I believe that the apostles and great saints in the Christian faith had their mind permanently changed so that they are more automatically inclined to think, according the goodness of God, under all circumstances.

When we work to become transformed, to have the Holy Spirit manifest inside of us at all times, then this way of thinking and being is also available to us. In order to go from sorrow to happiness and peace, using the tool of faith, we must first decide that we want to move from sorrow to faith and out of mourning and into contentment. The next step is to acknowledge and accept that it is not necessary for us to understand why everything, good or bad, occurs as it does. We release ourselves of the responsibility and the painful burden of ongoing investigation into the question of why events occurred, and the path that will only lead to more unanswerable questions and more pain. We recognize, like Job, that it is not our job to understand God's reasons for allowing things to happen and we simply agree to presume that all things occur for the good of God's plan. The final step is to simply surrender to God's will. We surrender to God's universe and live in the present moment by simply deciding to exercise and practice faith in the idea that God knows what He is doing. We can perform this final step by saying something like, "*Lord, I acknowledge the gift of life and experiences that you have given to me. I acknowledge that I don't know why these events have occurred and I now choose to believe that you have your reasons for exposing us to this experience and I choose to have faith in your decision to allow it to occur. I now move on, protected and held completely in your love into the present moment. I know that I am not alone and that not only are you with me but that I am also available to help others.*"

Having faith is a decision that you make to move on and respect God's plans. Having faith frees you from experiencing further grief and pain, and releases you from responsibility for what has happened, placing the responsibility back where it has always been from the beginning - with God. We must keep reminding ourselves that, in spite of our best intentions, ideas and actions, we are only co-creators of our lives, with God holding more cards that we have to work with. We must be able to accept the fact that our lives are always in a state of change, and that nothing remains the same forever. By accepting this fact we accept the very nature of the entire universe. Nothing remains the same, nor do people or even the thoughts and memories that we hold in our minds. We are all forever in a state of change and even after our death, our being continues to remain in a state of change. The vast majority of this change is not under our control.

Chapter 21: Overcoming guilt

When a perceived loss occurs, particularly losses that we are ourselves responsible for, we often do Lucifer's work for him by beating ourselves up. Again, by failing to forgive ourselves for our own faults, we play into Lucifer's hands by exerting our life energy against ourselves as we oppress and depress ourselves. It is key that we learn from our mistakes and get through the resultant pain, until the pain drains from us, so that we can use our energy for our family, friends and restitution. There is a kind of sorrow that results from loss that stems from poor decision making and our subsequent bad behavior. I have firsthand experience in that kind of sorrow from my own life. I have also seen it from interacting with prisoners whom I have coached, who are unwittingly oppressing and depressing themselves without realizing it. In 2nd Corinthians 7.10 the apostle Paul says, 'For the kind of sorrow God wants us to experience leads us away from sin [selfishness] and results in salvation. There's no regret for that kind of sorrow. But worldly sorrow, which lacks repentance, results in spiritual death."

In the United States, when someone is found guilty of a crime, or pleads to having committed a crime, regardless of the reasons, they are sentenced to extraordinarily punitive and lengthy jail terms. Obviously, in cases of murder, rape and other violent offenses, there is no choice but to incarcerate people for long periods of time in order to protect society from their behavior. From my experience in U.S. prisons, the lengths of incarceration imposed on non-violent, first time offenders are far too long and are so punitive that they actually can cause more harm than good. However, that is an entirely different subject about which I could write another book.

Suffice it to say that all those who are sentenced to jail and removed from society suffer tremendously, no matter how sanitary their imprisonment appears to be. Their families also suffer. In such a situation, victims of crimes have also suffered and many victims, authorities and other members of society alike appear to take pleasure in the suffering of those convicted. This is not a healthy attitude and it does not bring closure to victims or society. In fact, the false idea that closure for victims of crimes will occur upon the punishment of the criminal has lead to a kind of justification for lengthy sentences in cases where no prison terms are at all necessary once the offenders have learned their lesson. As such, society is ignorantly conditioned to believe that lengthy jail sentences lower the rates of crime, and that this is the cure for all crime. Statistics and studies show that lengthy and unnecessary incarceration does not help prevent crime and actually increases recidivism.

As it turns out psychologists are only now starting to confirm what Christ had already taught us over 2000 years ago. Forgiveness is the only real closure for victims of crimes. Forgiveness is the only tool that allows for people to evolve. In addition, for rehabilitation to be complete, criminals must also forgive themselves. It is not until victims can forgive the offenders that they are completely released from the burden of carrying a grudge against another human being. The forgiveness is not only good and necessary for the offender, but it is good and necessary for the total recovery of the victim.

The extreme situations that I have encountered with

people who are incarcerated is not unlike the situations faced by many ordinary people who are not in prison, or have never been to prison, but who still punish themselves every day in the same way. In prison the inmate typically feels sorrow for the suffering that he has caused the victims and for the suffering that he has imposed on his own family and friends. Most prisoners feel guilty because they may have caused loss and because they are not able to make restitution or provide for themselves, their families or their victims. Most prisoners who were not addicted to drugs while in prison or who were not mentally ill eventually come to terms with their crimes and are able to keep themselves from re-offending in the future after less than 6 months in jail. However, even in these cases, most prisoners continue to punish themselves with negative thoughts of their family's suffering. This cycle continues while they are in prison and in many cases even after they are released.

Chapter 22: Being an inspiration to others by developing yourself

By oppressing themselves in this way with their own thoughts, they incapacitate themselves from truly being able to help and inspire their family members or others while they are in prison by bettering themselves by any means. In many cases even after their release from prison the problem of self blame persists. While in prison many forget that they are still fathers, mothers, sons, brothers and friends even though they are in prison. There is always something that they can do to improve the lives of those outside of prison by simply maintaining a positive attitude and projecting that to their family and friends through phone calls, letters (in some cases e-mails) and during visitations.

Many prisoners imagine that their families are angry with them and wish that they are suffering in prison. In most of the cases that I have seen it is absurd to think that their family and friends actually spend time and energy hoping for the suffering of a loved one in prison. In other cases, however, it is true that society and even family members have been driven to the point where they do hope that the person in prison is suffering. However, in those extreme cases members of society and their family typically only want the person to change their negative thinking and behavior as described in 2 Corinthians 7.10, 10 (NLT), "For the kind of sorrow God wants us to experience leads us away from sin and results in salvation. There's no regret for that kind of sorrow. But worldly sorrow, which lacks repentance, results in spiritual death."

Blaming ourselves for things that have happened in the past is only productive until such time as we can find some new way of thinking that will prevent us from making the same mistakes again in the future. Once we've changed our thinking our behavior changes and it is no longer necessary for us to be locked into an energy draining cycle of self blame and self punishment. After a change of our minds it is necessary to forgive ourselves, request that God forgive us, and then focus on life in the present moment.

For those in prison, for soldiers at war, or for people who are parted from their families and loved ones for any reason, including death, it is essential that they not remain in sorrow indefinitely. Doing so may negatively affect their families and the lives of other people in the world, even if it is at a distance.

Chapter 23: Worry over what could have been

Many people engage in cycles of self oppression over far less important, perceived failures in their lives. They continue to revisit their past on a regular basis, blaming and punishing themselves for "what could have been", even though it is not clear that any element of their lives would have improved had their best plans been fulfilled in the past.

For those who have been convicted of crimes and who have been imprisoned, the experience itself, while undesirable, can result in spiritual enlightenment if they take advantage of the time that they have away from society, to engage in the study of spiritual writings and self improvement material. It becomes easy to recognize that God loves people enough to stop them in their tracks, and strip some out of society, so that they have the time to engage in self improvement through active study and practice of spiritual truths and texts. Thus, even prison can be a gift.

One cannot say whether or not the experience of prison or any other similar experience is good or bad until the event is over. From my own experience of my own imprisonment, my family grew closer together, my marriage was made stronger, my children were made stronger, and we were all drawn closer in our personal and collective relationships with God. And so for these reasons, even though prison is not a place I would choose to spend time, my personal experience of imprisonment was overall a positive experience because I took advantage of an amazing opportunity to study, learn and practice spiritual truths. Because of my efforts to connect with God, the time in prison was some of the most valuable in my life.

However, had I not forgiven myself, my prosecutors and oppressors, I would not have had the energy or inclination to remain a positive force for my family, every day, while I was in prison. I wrote to my family once a week, sent my children pictures from magazines and crafts that I made for them, and discussed spiritual and life issues with them daily, over the phone and during visitations. I remained a very active part of their lives, even though I was in prison. There is no such thing as a waste of time, only learning experiences. Events are not intrinsically good or bad but depend on how you treat them. Sometimes, through failure, our greatest potential is realized and we inspire people by our appreciation of life and how we stay happy in the present moment with God in spite of perceived failures.

Chapter 24: Perceived loss of the future

People can engage in worry and sorrow over the perceived loss of some potential future that they had been planning. This is even less useful. Worry about the loss of a potential future does not acknowledge the new possible futures that may be even greater than the one that we had formed in our imagination.

We say our "dreams are broken" when our reality does not meet our expectations. Again, our dreams are only highly valued ideas. They are not reality. They are not as valuable as what we already have in the present moment. Experiencing sorrow over the past or the future is the illness of not being able to appreciate what is available to us in the present moment. In this present moment we have everything that we need to be happy. We have air to breath, food to sustain us and a place to sleep. Our skin connects us to the entire universe; it does not separate us from it. We are part of everything.

Chapter 25: Sorrow caused by idealized ideas of how things "should be"

One of the most fundamental problems that human beings face is that they tend to value their ideas about reality more than they value reality itself. Our ideas of reality are not reality. I like to think of this as the fundamental human disease of the mind that was inflicted upon Adam and Eve when they ate the tree of knowledge of good and evil that forever left us attempting to judge everything according to what is desirable or undesirable. When we do this we fail to recognize the good that can come from undesirable events.

As Thich Nhat Hanh says, "They build up a self instead of letting go of the ideas of self then they look at this self as absolute truth and dismiss all other spiritual traditions as false. This is a very dangerous attitude; it always leads to conflicts and war. Its nature is intolerance." But as Christians (and for people of some other faiths, in particular Buddhism) part of our faith requires us to practice in every moment the letting go of our judging circumstances and submit to the events that God allows to occur and to focus on the goodness in them.

Dietrich Bonhoeffer (1906-1945) is one of the most well-known Christian theologians of the twentieth century. He was executed while in a prison camp during World War Two for opposing the Nazi's. In one of his letters to his fiancé, while he was looking forward to Christmas in a prison camp, Bonhoeffer captured this very idea that we do not really have true knowledge of good and evil in this excerpt: "And then, just when everything is bearing down on us to such an extent that we can scarcely withstand it, the Christmas message comes to tell us that all our ideas are wrong, and that what we take to be evil and dark is really good and light because it comes from God. Our eyes are at fault, that is all. God is in the manger, wealth in poverty, light in darkness, succor in abandonment. No evil can befall us; whatever men may do to us, they cannot but serve the God who is secretly revealed as love and rules the world and our lives."

Chapter 26: Letting go of the ideas that are the Ego

Our fundamental failure is that we believe in the false ideas about ourselves, and others, that are stored up and that create and form our ego or self image. Our only release from this painful cycle is to abandon our self image and our own ego by realizing that they are only ideas held in our brain. Once we realize that our entire ego and self image is a fictional character, created by ourselves, we can dispense with it altogether and stop spending our time and energy servicing the endless demands projected by our ego and we can instead choose freely what it is that we decide to do without any resistance from this phantom (our ego).

When we let go of the ideas held by ego our past becomes what it should have always been, memories, instead of what we perceive our experience to imply about ourselves (our ego or identity). Until one comes to this realization, one cannot have true freedom to love God, people, the universe and all of the creatures in it.

Until then the closest thing that we can hope to do is to identify as many of the false ideas that we cling to as a result of servicing our ego, our false self image, and false images of events.

The primary starting point to letting go of the ego is to work every day to dispense with each and every false idea, one at a time, and replace each with any higher level thought that brings us closer to the Kingdom of God than we were yesterday.

For those who are not yet ready and do not yet have the yearning and courage to abandon their self image and ego entirely, and live completely in the Holy Spirit, there is something else that can be done. We can and should pick away at the false construct of our ego piece by piece, every day, as we are called to do by the saints.

Chapter 27: Methods of living in the Way of Christ to experience joy and peace

I like to study religions and belief systems of the world, in particular Christianity, Zen Buddhism and Hindu. Zen Buddhism is, at its core, not a religion. The Buddha never claimed to be a God or the messiah. Buddha means "the awakened". Thus we can all be Buddhas by truly following and engaging with Christ, just as the celebrated Buddhist Thich Nhat Hanh practices Christianity. In Buddhism, Christ is recognized as a Buddha, because Christ is awakened .

Buddhism is the science and study of how to dispense with the ego and realize Nirvana, a condition of ultimate peace, by becoming "void" of the domination of our lives by the false self or ego. Use of the words, void and emptiness in Buddihism are often confused by Christians, who do not understand that the use of the words refers to being "void "and "empty" of domination by the ego, rather than being blank in the head and without intention at all. The void and emptiness sought by Buddhists is the same as the seeking of the freedom to make choices that are not being influenced by our physical and carnal (sinful) nature. As Christians, when we are not under the influence and domination of our earthly wants and desires, we are free to experience the fruits of this condition, which are true happiness and joy.

In Christianity we seek to have a relationship with God, in order to enable us to overcome our mental and physical desires that come from our imperfect egos and false thinking that is not congruent with the teachings of Christ and God. In Christianity we seek to obtain Nirvana and experience a life full of joy and peace by using Christ as our role model to help us to make decisions, overcome temptations and forgive us when we acknowledge our wrongdoing. Christians seek to maintain a life of peace, love, calm abiding and deep compassion for others, just as Christ, the apostles and saints asked us to do. I encourage Christians, who may have been misinformed about Zen Buddhism, to explore its teachings as an additional tool that can help people to live their lives more in alignment with the role model of Christ. For this I recommend Thich Nhat Hanh's book, "Living Buddha, Living Christ" as a good start and the series of books that are published every year called, "The Best Buddhist Writings of (the last year)" from which great wisdom can be gained on a variety of issues that every serious spiritual practitioner of Christianity also struggles with.

Achieving Nirvana is, for me, the same thing as allowing the Holy Spirit to come upon us by disassembling and letting go of the ego, which is the collective set of ideas that creates the false personality that prevents the Holy

Spirit from uniting with us completely. Our own ideas and beliefs about who we are (our personality) is really the greatest barrier that prevents many people from fully integrating with the Holy Spirit, and receiving the fruits of the spirit, joy, peace and fulfillment.

For me achieving Nirvana is an experience that we are all capable of, that changes our thinking and our lives forever. It fills us with the Holy Spirit, instead of with our constructed ego. The Holy Spirit keeps us in a state of bliss, no matter what feelings we experience. The Bible calls for us to do the same thing; to die and to be reborn again. What is to die is our ego and self image, which, no matter how nice it may appear, is a falsehood that causes selfish intentions to manifest in sin, and forces us to do what we would not decide to do otherwise. When we are reborn we can still make mistakes, however, we still have access to the same forgiveness that we required before when we were being led and coerced by our ego. When we are reborn the apostle Paul says that we receive the Holy Spirit and our 'thinking is changed.'

Chapter 28: Transformation and the experience of the presence of God

I can attest that I have had such transformations in my own life, and they have been the most beautiful gifts that I have ever received. God continues to sustain me in a state of bliss whenever I make the presence of God the focus of my daily life. While I still experience feelings, just like any other human being, I am not a slave to them, and I can convert the energy of the feelings to do the good that the will of God compels from us as best as I can understand and study what I believe God's will may be. I have transcended feelings and I am no longer their servant.

I see, access and use the entire spectrum of the energy from sorrow to joy as useful energy whenever they occur. For me God's will is simple. Mark 12.29, "Love God with all your heart, and Love others as though they were yourself." That is all God really asks for us to do. We don't need to do anything else. We don't need to make money or have possessions or fame or political power.

Saint Augustine (354-430 A.D.) described his own total transformation (his achieving of Nirvana), in which he dispensed with his own ego and received the grace and bliss provided by God through the Holy Spirit. In excerpts from his "Confessions" he states, "My inner self was a house divided against itself." St. Augustine describes how his decisions to do God's will and even more simple things involving acts of self control where thwarted by some enemy within, which I view as the energy from his ego or self image. St. Augustine goes on to describe his battles with himself in his mind and feelings, which took place until he was released completely from the bondage of his own ego. Release from his ego made way for the bliss and clarity of thinking, that comes from the Holy Spirit, to fill his heart, and which subsequently eliminated any other resistance from his mind and ego, whenever he decided any further courses of action in his life.

St. Augustine describes his emancipation from the enslavement of himself to the false constructs and images of his ego, and the death of his ego, in the same why that Zen Buddhist masters describe their own instant experience of Kensho, Satori or Nirvana. "For in an instant, as I came to the end of the sentence, it was as though the light of the confidence flooded into my heart and all the darkness of doubt was dispelled. I marked the place in my [Bible] with my finger and closed the book. You converted me to yourself, so that I no longer placed any hope in this world but stood firmly upon the rule of faith."

Chapter 29: Experience of loss can lead to enlightenment

While each person who succeeds in achieving this state of enlightenment has arrived at it through a different set of experiences, the attainment is usually precipitated by great desire and sometimes comes from great need to alleviate suffering. Even people who are not spiritual have been able to achieve this experience. I believe that this is because, as Christ said, the laws of God are written on all of our hearts, and the scriptures say that God will still also judge those people who do not know Jesus, yet still do God's will. Some people have even experienced the instant abandonment of ego and a direct encounter with the Holy Spirit that enabled them to cope with some extreme experience, including great trauma that occurred while being victimized during a violent crime, during mental or physical torture, in association with a near death experience, or in relation to some other extreme experience.

The point is that the experience is available to us all and I believe it is more easily accessible to those who seek, with great determination, a communion with God (seek and you shall find). God and Jesus then determine who will enter the Kingdom.

Chapter 30: Think on that which is good

In principal the process for transforming any undesirable state of mind into a more desirable state of mind, that maintains us in the Kingdom of God, is fundamentally the same. In the Bible, God and Jesus call upon us to come to, and remain in, the Kingdom of God today, and every day. Not just in some far off distant future when we die, but today   .

The Lord's Prayer says it best. "Thy Kingdom Come, Thy will be done on Earth, as it is in Heaven." This is a clear call to manifest the Kingdom of God here, today. It is clear from the Scriptures that God does not want us to suffer today and wait for our suffering to be relieved sometime in the future. In Luke 6.20-26, Jesus says, "Blessed are you who weep now for you will laugh ... for surely your reward is great in heaven." And where is this heaven? Matthew 10.7 and many other scriptures tells us that the "Kingdom of Heaven has come." 2 Corinthians 6.2 says, "Today is the day of salvation." St. Augustine said, "Why not now?"

I believe that Jesus was able to release people from the domination of their eco, which allowed them to become filled with the Holy Spirit in the past, and he continues to enable this today. While we may still experience evil thoughts and selfish feelings, we need not be enslaved to them if we seek out the Holy Spirit, and place the Spirit in control of our lives.

Chapter 31: Tools and the power of participating in a group

How then can we remain in the Kingdom of God, when faced with the perception of loss or sorrow? If you believe in God and seek to live in the one true Way of Christ then there are many techniques and tools to help you live in the Way. Obviously there is the Bible, churches, groups, sanghas and there are the writings of the Apostles, Saints and Christian practitioners. Other tools that can be of use in your Christian or spiritual walk include psychology, Zen Buddhism and even contemplation of some of the ways of thinking that come from the study of other religions.

I encourage you to make an ongoing study of the methods by reading books and watching educational films on overcoming suffering. I would also encourage you to attend groups and clubs where other people also struggle with the same issues that you struggle with. Preferably groups and clubs that are based in spiritual principals that are in alignment with your own faith. God intended for us to come together in groups. In this writing I am sharing some of my own favorite methods for overcoming loss and grief. Some I have developed on my own, and some I have borrowed from others whom I will name.

At first any process requires practice until it becomes our default natural behavior, as it has become in those people who we call saints and sages. Anyone can become a saint or a sage if they are willing to dispense with their own limited way of thinking and being to rather adopt that which is valuable to God, as described in the Bible and religious texts.

We know in great detail what the Bible asks for us to do, including thinking on that which is good, but our ego resists and we cannot become saints or sages until we surrender completely to the will of God. That means that we must surrender our fate to God as God expresses his will to us in the form of everyday events, whether we desire them or not, and that are out of our control. We will not be delivered from suffering in our lives until we can completely forgo our own desires of the mind and flesh and rid our minds of our own false thinking and false ego, making our minds completely available to God.

Chapter 32: The process from oppression and depression to joy and peace

Here is one of my own baseline methods for changing the false thinking that leads to oppression and depression. The goal is to replace our default thoughts with the thinking that God intended for us have, so that we can enjoy our lives and the universe that God has gifted to us.

1. Do not resist pain and suffering, let it flow through you and release itself. Be with the feelings until they are completely released. Harness the energy from the feelings while you are experiencing them if you can. Let out your feelings in a safe manner with consideration for others. Example: "I am experiencing fear. What does

this feel like? To what positive use can I put this energy of fear? Perhaps I can use it to connect with God in the present moment." Consciously set and agree with yourself on a timeline by which you will end your process of mourning so as to not stay trapped inside of the process endlessly. In some cultures a period of mourning is as little as two weeks.

2. Ask yourself if there is anything that you need to change about yourself, and/or forgive yourself for, in order to keep from continuing to experience the pain, suffering and loss again, and work on making these changes, 2 Corinthians 7.10 (NLT) "For the kind of sorrow God wants us to experience leads us away from sin and results in salvation. There's no regret for that kind of sorrow. But worldly sorrow, which lacks repentance, results in spiritual death."

3. Identify specific ideas or memories that are causing you to suffer and feel pain and change your thinking in respect to those memories and ideas. 2 Corinthians 10.5, "We take every thought captive and make it obedient to Christ."

4. Remember that our ideas about the past, present and future realities are not necessarily absolute fact. Therefore avoid latching onto ideas that cause you further oppression and prolong the process of mourning.

1 Corinthians 13.9-10, "Now our knowledge is partial an incomplete and even the gift of prophecy reveals only part of the whole picture! But when full understanding comes, these partial things will become useless.'

5. We must acknowledge that unexplainable and undesirable events, like natural disasters that kill our loved ones, are not punishments against ourselves personally, but that God may have chosen us to help reveal his glory through overcoming our suffering. We must also acknowledge that it is not necessary for us to know the answers to the question of "why" God allows things to happen. Remember Job 38- 42, wherein God asks Job, "Who is it this that questions my wisdom with such ignorant words? ... 40. Do you still argue with the Almighty? You are God's critic, but do you have the answers?" If we do need an answer to the question "why" then consider Jesus' answer as to why a blind man was afflicted with blindness in John 9, "It was not because of his sins or his parents' sins... This happened so that the power of God could be seen..." Look deeply into what good things will result from bad events.

6. Choose to release any attachment to the thought or idea that oppresses us. If necessary replace the oppressive thoughts, ideas or memories with good thoughts that make us feel good. Don't run from them using crutches like drugs or alcohol; face them and

replace them. Example: "I choose not to oppress myself with that thought." If thinking of a loved one who died, dwell on the joy derived from your experience with them when they were alive, rather than on any suffering that they may have experienced during the time leading up to their death. Remember no-one is alone at the time of their death, God is with them. If someone is away from you, meditate on them and wish them love and peace, and remember the good times. Philippians 4.8 "Fix your thoughts on what is true, and honorable, and right, and pure, and lovely and admirable. Think about things that are excellent and worthy of praise. Keep putting into practice all you have learned..."

7. Chose to remain in the present moment. In the present moment, we don't think about painful memories of the past or worry with fear about what may happen in the future. Rather we experience the miracle of the experience of life itself right now. Right now we are in God's hands and we live in Christ. Right now is a refuge. Right now all futures are possible and all pasts are not relevant. Matthew 6.19, "25. That is why I tell you not to worry about everyday life ...27. Can all your worries add a single moment to your life?" Philippians 4.6, "Don't worry about anything; instead pray about everything. Tell God what you need, and thank him for all he has done. Then you will experience God's peace, which exceeds anything we can understand. His peace

will guard your hearts and minds as you live in Christ."

8. Remember that there is a balance in the universe and that experiencing undesirable events will increase your entitlement of desirable events, joy, love and happiness. Luke 6:20-26, "Blessed are you who weep now, for you will laugh." The processes above are what I believe we are called to do at all time if we are practicing our Christianity. We thank God instead of blaming God. We become the lights and the Glory of God when Lucifer strikes at us. Thus we abide in the Love of God and we spread and share that Love and compassion with all living beings.

Chapter 33: Refuge in the present moment

I would like to share with you ways to live in the present moment, which I believe is the best way to alleviate all suffering and perceived sorrow from loss. What does living in the present moment look like? Consider what would happen if your memory was erased and you were unable to recall memories that oppress and depress you. In that moment, everything would be new to you and alive and we would be like children (just like Christ tells us that in order to enter his Kingdom we must become like children).

Children don't have huge egos that are false ideas about who they are, what they should be and how they should react to every situation. Children have so much energy because they are not using their energy to carry around and service an entire rule set and set of beliefs that makes up their ego. We experience great excitement every day around children and even those people with handicaps that cause their memory to be lost, because we get to witness their enjoyment and experience of commonplace events as though it was their first time. The joy that life in the present moment brings to them also brings joy to our hearts because we remember what it was like to not have the burden of an ego.

Similarly, because the future represents unlimited potential for children and for some handicapped people, the future is an exciting place where failure is not feared and perhaps not even recognized. This is living in the present moment. Being void of attachments to reliving painful memories or attachments to ways of being that are designed to protect us against possible future and present failures. In this moment we can find true peace. When we are not living in the future or the past or into some constructed image of how we should act (the ego) then we can be appreciative of every single moment and we move from being the "sufferer" to the "experience" itself.

When we are fully present we are not escaping. In fact it is just the opposite. We are being fully present to everything that is happening around us. Instead of trying to interpret reality we become part of it, just as it is part of us, and we simply allow the light, the smells, the tastes, the sounds and the sensations to come to us. We are not straining to taste, smell or feel, we are just one with the experience right where we are without any distractions coming from the voices, busyness and interpretations that are normally creating noise and chatter in our own minds. It is this incessant chatter, talking and analysis of our interiorized self or ego, that has its uses, but in most cases is just interfering with our own direct experience of reality. It is nice for us to be able to choose to turn off these inner voices and chatter when we decide.

Imagine your mind in a condition where it is not "processing" and "interpreting" or "speaking" to you but it is just listening without struggling to make meaning out of everything. When we are in this condition of openness, not blocking what is happening to us, colors, smells, sounds, sensations are more vibrant. You see things that you've never noticed before, you feel a great weight lifted off of you, and a restoration of energy. Imagine the luxury of not having to even have an opinion. Your actions are still guided by your intentions (hopefully you've decided to do good as discussed earlier). You are not brain dead, you are just allowing the experience of what is around you to enrich you rather than tax you.

It is fair to say that while I was in prison I did often, intentionally, close my eyes and relive some of the happier experiences from my past in my mind in order to help cope with the passage of time away from my loved ones. I will always cherish the memory of my daughter laying on my chest when she was 3 years old, while we were napping at a playground in a quiet and breezy public park. I had many other great memories that I would relive; ones with my wife, my son and others. I would sometimes close my eyes and create brand new realities, pasts and futures with my family and friends in wonderful places. Being a coach, and knowing about the hazards of becoming too attached to the past or idealized futures, I would not let myself get too carried away with my sessions of past memories. In the end I would start to convert the energy from those past memories and other realities into thoughts of love and joy and peace that I would project to my family members, wherever they were.

Using my memories and imagination was of utility from time to time, and using the methods of becoming completely present in the moment was even more effective in strengthening my connection with my loved ones, even though they were not physically present. When you are truly in the present moment you become aware of the fact that you are connected with everything, right now. You are connected with the water in the streams in the mountains, you are connected with the sunlight and the grass and the trees, and you are most certainly directly connected with your loved ones, even though you don't see them in front of you. You are sharing the same space with them. When you are in the present moment there is a knowing and an overwhelming sensation that your skin is not separating you from the world and the universe but it is connecting you to it.

When you are in the present moment the entire universe and everything and everyone in it becomes smaller, small enough to fit into a single idea in your mind. Thus there is no "out there" and "in here", there is only "here".

Chapter 34: Being present during both desirable and undesirable experiences

I have come to experience that being fully present in the moment places me into a state of peace even when I am going through an undesirable experience where the outcomes are uncertain. When I was in prison there were many times when the location where I was being placed and held, and what was being required of me, was out of my control. Some difficult times included the requirement to do work that I did not feel like doing or at times when I did not feel like doing it, being forced to remain locked in small cells for hours, or being in the company of people that I found challenging to be around, and many other experiences. In those situations, I coped with them in several different ways such as asking myself, "what was in this moment for me to get," and "how can I reach out to others and be of help and support to them for what they are going through."

One of the most powerful techniques to help me to be at peace in the most extreme circumstances is to simply let whatever is going to happen occur, without my resistance, and being part of the entire experience by being 100% in the present moment. I do not distract myself with my own analysis and appraisal of every situation in which I find myself. If I was in shackles preparing to board a flight on "Con-Air", or in an elevator with dangerous criminals who were getting ready to fight each other, I was able to remain at peace, ambivalent to whatever happened, accepting it and being with it. Other people sensed this peace that I had, and it affected them in a positive way. I rarely found myself being challenged by anyone. Most people that I met wanted me to show them how they too could find this peace and child like joy that I seemed to have without the use of any drugs, even while I was in prison.

It really all boils down to just being able to be quiet in one's mind, and listen instead of interpreting. Becoming present to the quality of each breath is a way to snap into the present moment at anytime. For example I can count how many repetitions of something would happen on my in-breath and my out-breath. I can take a few steps and count the number of steps I was taking on my in-breath and my out-breath. I can observe the quality of my breath, whether my breath is being drawn in from the muscles in my chest or it is being drawn in from the muscles in my abdomen. I would notice the differences in the sensations of my body in relation to my breath. On each in-breath I would analyze where the muscles in my body felt tired or strained, and on each out-breath I would consciously release the strain. You can consciously relax yourself and feel as though you just had a massage by simply asking your own muscles to relax in the specific areas where you need for them to rest.

Chapter 35: We already have everything we need to be happy

In every moment we already have all that we need to be happy. We have the air to breath, food to eat, a place to sleep and we have the gifts of God. We have our emotional energy, love, happiness, excitement, and even fear and pain. Fear and pain should not be our enemies because they are part of all of the sensations of life. We have the trees, grass, birds, insects, animals, people and the clouds painting the sky. Nothing remains the same from day to day. When we look at life this way, then life is beautiful. We are energized and electrified by all of the colors and sensory inputs of the present moments that are available to us in the here and now, every single instant of every single day. A simple walk, or a simple drink of water, or some tea, becomes an exciting gift. This was all true for me, even in the darkest prison cells, from where I sat being totally present, and from inside, which I reached out using my consciousness, to share peace, love and joy with others.

Only when we allow our worry about yesterday and tomorrow to manifest do we spoil the present joy of our moments. There is a miracle in this moment and every moment because of the fact that we are alive. Doctors, poets and theologians can describe all the functions of our hearts, but only God knows exactly what causes it to beat. Our breath, our heartbeat, and our lives are a gift from God. The fact that we know little about the details of where we come from, why we are here, or where we are going, should make us all the more comfortable about not knowing everything, and more appreciative of what we do have in every breath of the mystery of life. Some things are not meant for us to know and that is beautiful in itself.

Chapter 36: Joy and excitement about not knowing everything

What an amazing miracle life is. What a gift it is that we are not the ones who are responsible for having to make the sun rise every day and to feed all the people, creatures and plants in the world.

When unpredicted things happen I don't worry about them. It's not my job to guarantee the success of every outcome, of every business and every project that I undertake, and so I am not afraid to fail. I am more afraid of not having tried. I often joke to my friends that I am sticking around just to see what happens next because life is so exciting, because we don't have the answers to these questions. How boring our lives might be if we did know everything about the past and the future into which we are going. There would be less gained from watching a movie that we already saw.

So what can we do to be in the present moment? Think back to your own earlier memories from when you were a child. I can remember playing with my friends, playing late into the night during some holidays, and how all the colors of the lights at night seemed so vibrant and how exciting it was just to be out in the crisp air and blue light. Why was it all so exciting? Because I was closer to the Holy Spirit then than I was at some later times in my life.

I've had to work to unwind most of my adult thinking and misconceptions in order to be able to appreciate every moment again to a similar degree as to what I did as child. Once again I have become as a child by throwing away my own ego through meditation, study, prayer, and the constant desire to maintain a relationship with God, and be present at every moment throughout every day. Now, once again, I feel the vibrancy of life in every moment, and I also have my memories of my life and experiences that I take with me.

I do not mean to say that I now live my entire life in the present moment and I am always void of the ego. There are some people who make this shift permanently either by accident or desire and there is nothing wrong with that. In my case I am a human being subject to the entire experience of mind, body and soul. What is important to me is that I continue to get better at being able to shift my consciousness into the present moment whenever I like, and I now know that this is a skill that everyone has the ability to develop and use to experience happiness, joy and peace, as well as many other positive sensations and effects.

When I talk about being a child I do not mean that we

should not learn from our experience or be selfish. I mean we should be open to life and be able to be 100% present whenever we choose. I don't need to erase my memory to practice being in the present moment, I simply need to recognize that ideas and thoughts are raining down into my head at all times when I am conscious, and even when I am asleep. I need to make a habit of not becoming attached to any particular thoughts or ideas. I can keep my memories, but, in order for me to be happy it is not necessary for me to keep reliving past memories, or to become attached to any new ideas or new potential futures that come into my imagination.

Chapter 37: Avoid being stuck on the future

Some people find it hard to not be thinking of something or to be attached to any thoughts or memories. The problem with attachments to good ideas and memories is that thinking about them too often may prevent you from new experiences that you could otherwise be having in the present moment.

In the present moment the universe is spraying a fire hose of beautiful experiences at you and you might not even know it if you are living in your mind. For those people who have not yet developed mindfulness to the degree that they can simply stop thinking about ideas, then I recommend that the next best thing is to focus on thinking about good things as the Apostle Paul tells us in 2 Corinthians 10.5 (NLT) "...We capture their rebellious thoughts and teach them to obey Christ," and Philippians 4.8, (NLT), "... Fix your thoughts on what is true, and honorable, and right, and pure, and lovely, and admirable. Think about things that are excellent and worthy of praise."

If you are stuck thinking on ideas about the future then allow yourself the possibility for failing to attain your future goals without becoming depressed. It is important to remember that we are responsible for less than 10% of what is happening in the totality of reality in any given moment and as such, the normal machinations of the universe may cause us to fail to attain future goals, no matter how good the goals are, and no matter how hard we work.

I believe that it is prudent to work hard on things that you take up, but not so hard that your life becomes unbalanced. Consider the possibility of predestination. Sometimes it is required that we acknowledge that if something is meant for us to achieve then it will happen, regardless of how much we work.

We must avoid becoming attached to what we do not yet have. For that matter we must avoid becoming attached to the idea that we have anything other than life itself.

Remember we are only passing through life. Everything we have today is made out of constituents that were here before we came and that will remain in some form after we leave. I prefer to travel light and not become attached to ideas or things.

Chapter 38: Do not grasp too tightly onto what is changing

It is a great experience to give and to receive love from people and other creatures, but we should avoid grasping too tightly to what is alive because everything that is alive is ever changing and impermanent. No matter how much we love our spouse or children we must remember that we do not OWN them, and even the relationships from which we experience love, peace and joy today may not continue in the same form as we would like in the future. It is perfectly acceptable and necessary to take a stand for ourselves and our loved ones, while also being able to acknowledge that we are not in complete control.

These are good reasons to appreciate the moments now with our loved ones. Simply be aware it is the propensity of our human natures to become attached to oppressive thoughts. Choose instead to think about what is good. This is what God calls us to do in virtually every faith, including Christianity. As you become better at thinking about what is good, then focus your attention to looking deeply into what is good in this present moment. This can be done through simply practicing being in the moment by observing your breathing.

For example, while you are walking you can count the number of steps you take in each exhalation and each inhalation. You can become present by enjoying a nice cup of your favorite beverage or by just looking carefully into the things around you and appreciating the beauty in the fact that we know little of where anything came from nor exactly where it is all going. You can become present by taking a walk and focusing on your breathing, your favorite trees and the fact that God has arranged that the sky will be repainted with clouds over and over again so that it is never the same picture.

I frequently take great pleasure in looking into the secret life among blades of grass, and the ants that live in the grass. The ants know how to be present, just like other animals and our pets. In the mind of an ant I imagine there must exist great pleasure because their little ant minds are always in the present moment and they do not appear to have the capacity to worry about the past or future. The little ants have peace that is available to all of us larger creatures, if we practice appreciating every single moment, and avoid attaching oppressive thoughts to ourselves and our environment.

Chapter 39: Decide not to think about oppressive thoughts and ideas

We are the only ones that oppress ourselves with our own thinking. The key to being in the present moment is to realize that we have a choice as to what we think about. We have a choice whether or not we will oppress ourselves with ideas and memories OR to decide NOT to oppress ourselves with specific thoughts, memories or ideas. We have a choice to trade wrong thinking for happy memories, ideas, thoughts or courses of action. We have a choice to place ourselves into direct experience now, that bring us into the present moment, to enjoy the feast of light, color, sound and sensation that is available to us at all times, and that is provided to us by God.

Remember that when we experience undesirable events and the associated, undesirable feelings that come with them, that we are called by God to go through these circumstances, and suffer these feelings, in a way that enables us to experience the Glory of God. If we want to experience ecstasy from tragedy, then we have to take action. We have to become a participant in the expression of the Glory of God by discerning the positive from the negative.

Magnets have both a North Pole and a South Pole. If

you cut a magnet into two pieces you end up with two new smaller pieces each having a North Pole and a South Pole. For centuries, science has tied to synthesize a mono-pole magnet, which is a magnet that consists of only a North Pole or a South Pole. We can use our imagination to create a mono-pole magnet in our mind. We can imagine that it might look like a circular piece of metal that only attracts South Poles of other magnets.

Just as in the case of our imagined magnet that we are unable to create in the physical world, we can visualize it in our minds, using the gift of our minds given by God. This imagination that is given to us as a gift is capable of being used against us to make what is neither good nor bad appear to us as bad and depressing.

What we are called to do as Christians is to move towards God and the Kingdom of Heaven. So while the universe may appear to have an equal number of desirable and undesirable events God and Jesus offer us the possibility of creating a mono-pole of joy, peace and love in our own minds, using the power of our imagination. We still feel the sensations of pain and sorrow as we continue to feel sensations of joy and happiness; however we transcend these sensory emotions and remain in bliss, choosing to focus on all goodness that can be derived from every event. We take solace in knowing that nothing ever really goes away - it only changes form.

Chapter 40: There is no shame in NOT suffering

It is my sincere hope that the passages of this text on dealing with loss cause you to change your thinking, and to experience peace, contentment joy, and help you to appreciate and experience the Glory of God. It is important to avoid the temptation to feel guilty or unusual because you are no longer being oppressed by the same ideas and mourning processes as the other people around you. Feeling warmth, love and bliss while others are in sorrow does not make you a cold robot; it just makes you transcendent over your thoughts and emotions via the Spirit.

Even though I partake of the bliss of God, I am still a human being and my first reaction is to also experience sadness, but my sadness does not last as long as others because I automatically cease judging the situation, and start seeing what good can come, and what I can to do be part of the experience of good and manifestation of the glory of God.

Nowadays my baseline emotions typically convert into compassion for others much more rapidly than happens for most people. I see people in their sorrow, and that in itself makes me feel empathy for them. You should not feel guilty for feeling complete with what is naturally occurring, according to the will of God, and nor should you allow others to make you feel guilty for not feeling sorry.

Again, one of the biggest benefits of being a Christian is to be comforted, just as Jesus stated in Matthew 11.28, "Come to me, all of you who are weary and carry heavy burdens, and I will give you rest. Take my yoke upon you. Let me teach you, because I am humble and gentle at heart, and you will find rest for your souls."

Chapter 41: Consideration and compassion for the suffering of others

If reading this text does lead you to transcend the feelings of sorrow and loss, you should not try to also force others to mourn, grieve and experience the absence of sorrow in the same way that you have. You can share this text with others and see if they are interested. You can share some of the ideas with them if they are receptive, but you must avoid making anyone feel wrong for failing to dispense with their own sorrow and depression, just as you don't want to be told how you should feel.

I recently read an article that said that the number one complaint from those who are suffering the loss of a loved one, particularly parents who suffer the loss of a child, is that other people are not suffering or mourning the same way that they do. Apparently people have very specific attachments to the ideas of how others should suffer and what others should do to mourn along with them. While this is not an issue of being right or wrong, it is something to keep in mind in our relationships with our loved ones.

It is important to ask our loved ones about how they are suffering and ask them if there is anything that you can do to help them through their own mourning. If their requests are reasonable then join them in their mourning and do as they ask, but do not do so begrudgingly or it defeats the purpose of enabling them to exhaust the energy of their own sorrow. You can learn a great deal by participating in mourning with others and you don't have to be in sorrow yourself in order to participate in mourning. When trying to be there for others your ability to be patient is important. If you say you don't have enough patience then consider it an opportunity to learn how to have more. Too many people make up reasons, that are not really justifiable, to avoid spending time or giving resources to helping others in cases where they actually could.

One way to participate in the expression and experience of the Glory of God is to decide to overcome sorrow and pain, and then to help others to overcome their own sorrow and pain. Just taking this course of action can cause great joy to appear where once there was only great suffering. However, don't expect others to be so easily able to liberate themselves from suffering. There are a variety of reasons why people may feel obligated to mourn and be depressed, including culture, family teachings and even religion. Whether or not their expression of suffering is wrong or right in your opinion, you will never help someone to release their own sorrow by attempting to make them feel wrong for suffering. Again when it comes to ways of life there is no wrong or right there is only living.

Chapter 42: The practice of compassion

If you are strong enough, and if you have overcome the suffering yourself, and if you can keep your loved ones from pushing you back into a relapse of depression by keeping these teachings alive within your mind, then you can make yourself available to help reduce the suffering of loved ones and others. In order to do so you must practice Love according to 1 Corinthians 13, as in, "Love is patient, love is kind, Love is not boastful, proud or rude, love does not demand its own way and it does not keep record of past wrongs."

You must be forgiving, as in, Matthew 18.21, willing to forgive over and over again. Above all do not brag about how good you fee in the face of some event that is the cause of great suffering for others. If you imagine the sorrow that someone experiences as a large breath of air that they take into their lungs and the amount of guilt or resistance that they have in releasing the air in their lungs as the constricting of their wind pipe, then you can imagine that some people may be able to expel the air of sorrow quickly, while others may take years to expel the same amount of sorrow.

The most important way to support your loved ones through suffering and/or guilt is to be patient and forgiving of the time, energy and resources that this will consume. Part of the practice of compassion is to look deeply into, and investigate the suffering being experienced by the loved one, and ask them to tell you how they are suffering. Then listen actively, with patience. Even if you disagree with what they are sharing you must realize that they believe what they are saying.

By listening and even inviting them to share their stories of pain and suffering you can draw out some of the air of sorrow from their lungs. Even though you may not agree with everything that they are saying, you learn how you can best react in the future, and be there for them in the future in a way that will best help them to alleviate and expel the breath of sorrow.

You may find a better way to react. This takes great patience, and you may hear things that you don't agree with, and perhaps even have to endure criticism of yourself. In light of all that you hear - good or bad, nice or ugly - it is important to not attempt to make them wrong, but rather to acknowledge what they are going through. By acknowledging you can join them in their place of suffering and then help them to make a plan for the future that will get them out of suffering by planting seeds.

Once you join them where they are by patiently listening to them, then you respect them and earn their trust, and you can plant the seeds of flowers that will bloom where they are, and bring them out of suffering. You can create hope in them for the future or the present by saying things, such as, "boy isn't it good that we had this person while we did and that now they are with God..." or " how much fuller our lives will be now and in the future since we can continue on in a new way thanks to..."

Chapter 43: The importance of love, forgiveness and hope

Compassion enables us to get what someone is going through, and to help them to reach a higher level. It is not condemning and making wrong. Love is love, it is patient and kind, and it does not demand its own way, and it perseveres. Forgiveness enables us to forgive someone for attacking us when they are in the pit of their own suffering, without even having to tell them that we forgive them.

Hope eliminates the need and burden for us to be successful at everything. Love has the courage to ask to be forgiven even when it is right. You can be this love, this patience, this perseverance, this understanding, this forgiving, and this hope as an expression of the Glory of God. You can turn sorrow into ecstasy and love for God.

Chapter 44: Putting it all together

If we love God and truly practice faith, how can we say that anything is ever a loss? If even what we perceive as a great evil is somehow being counterbalanced, and even overpowered, with the great good from God. How can we not be comforted in the presence and plan that God has for us, that will bring all of those who suffer to experience joy, peace and the Glory of God by means that only God himself can conceive. We have lost nothing; we have been given everything, including experiences of love, joy, and of pain and sorrow, with other people, and in various places with various things. We experience time and everything in it. Without the experience of sorrow we have no contrast to use to determine what experiences are joyful. In this way pain and joy go together and are both necessary.

We experience time as the transition from one thought and experience to another. The past does not leave us, it is always being integrated into us as we experience it. It nourishes us, and the positive energies and people that we've experienced and assimilated are accessible to us at any time, no matter where we are, no matter what objects surround us, or do not surround us. We are the source of the love that we experience and have experienced in the past, just as we are the source of the suffering that we visit on ourselves by neglecting the present moment, running away from God, and our practice of the teachings of Christ.

We are thrown into every moment. We are different in every moment as we go through time and each thought that we have just had. By living completely in the present we don't need to worry about losing anything or having lost anything. All we need to be happy is already here, and all we have experienced is already here in this present moment, integrated into our being. It is critical that we forgive ourselves and others for the past, that we relieve ourselves from burden of worrying what we may discover in the future, and guilt that we did not make the best decisions that we could have made.

Let the practice of HOPE for the realizations of our plans

for the future replace our rigid and unforgiving expectations for the future. We must continue to remind ourselves that life is collaboration between ourselves, what we would like to manifest, and what God intends for us to experience and manifest.

It is essential for our well being, joy and happiness that we do not cling too tightly to what is alive and changing every day. We must not fall into the illusion that we can have complete control over the future or anything else. The fact is that we have very little control over even this very moment. All we have any control over is our own reactions. Everything is in a state of flux at all times. Nothing is permanent. This is not a bad thing. Be thankful to God that nothing is permanent. In all experiences, be grateful to God as we live within the domain of God. What harm can ever come to any of us if, even after death, we remain within the realm of God?

My own story

My knowledge about overcoming loss comes from the experience in my own life, and from my own efforts to cope with situations that were extraordinary to me. My goal is to share what I learned to be true for myself in the hope that it will help others. To help achieve my goals it may be of some interest for readers to know a little about my background. I will do my best to keep my life story as brief as possible since my history is not crucial in understanding the main body.

I am the youngest of three bothers born a Christian. I lived through some difficult experiences as a child since my father was physically abusive, and my parents divorced when I was 5 years old. My mother, brothers and I moved around the United States initially to avoid my father. I think the experience encouraged us to gental spirits. On thing that I did have access to no matter what our financial situation was good private schooling, which my mother made sure that we received no matter were we lived. And I believe that good education has really helped me in my life and my brothers and I all did well in our studies. Some time during my high school years my father reconciled with my brothers and me, and to some extent, with my mother. Limited relations were re-established. He apologized to me for the things that had happened. Eventually we visited each other often, and had a more beneficial relationship. Later in my 30's we even worked together occassionaly in some business ventures from time to time. Many of these business dealings left me disappointed and with the realization that I needed to do business in a different way than my father. I began to realize what the Bible scriptures are talking about when they refer to overcoming the negative inheritance of our family. I love and forgive my father and always will and I also recognize what traits from him I must overcome and guard against in my own life. Fortunately I have the love and grace of Jesus Christ and my father in Heaven to help me in these tasks.

In terms of significant osses in my own life, like many other people I have experienced the death of loved ones.

The most significant for me was the loss of my eldest brother Steve in 1999, who died from an overdose of prescription medication. He was found in his apartment by my mother two days after his death and their remains an air of mystery surrounding his death. To make matters worse after his body was removed unbeknownst to our family many of his most valuable and significant possessions were stolen from his apartment. While the loss was significant for me, I can't imagine how difficult it was for my mother particularly with all of his most important personal effects being removed. I acknowledge her for managing through her greif. The sorrow of her loss still lingers to this day. A great deal of what I have learned and share in this book is a direct result of my experiences in trying to help my mother in dealing with the loss of my brother.

Another significant loss was that of my father, which occurred during a very difficult time in my own life, while I was living in South Africa and my business was failing. I was unable to see him in the hospital in the United

States before his death. Because of other subsequent events I was unable to attend his funeral. Even at the time of the writing of this book, which is over 9 years after his death, I have been physically restrained from making the trip to see his grave. This is something that I have yet to do.

At the age of 16, I had the traumatic experience of having to give that child up for adoption because the mother and I were too young to care for him. We both really wanted that child to have the best chance in life that we both knew that we could not provide for him. As a result of this experience there were many years when I felt that it was my responsibility to live an exemplary life so that if the boy ever wanted to meet me I could not only be of some use to him and some encouragement. IT was an open adoption and a few years ago I made myself available to him if he would ever like to reach out to me and I am hopeful that he will reach out sometime just so that we can meet each other.   I hope that he is doing well in his life and it was hard to give up a child.

I have suffered through 3 failed marriages in my life. Obviously, I had a role in the loss of these relationships, but the pain of each of these experiences had a major impact on me and is worth mentioning. Thanks to God and to some extent my failures in the other relationships, I am happily married today for over 13 years, and I have two wonderful children.

Six months after my brother died, when I was 29, I lost a kidney in a motor cross racing accident that prevented me from engaging in the sport. Then I almost died in the hospital from a blod clot in my leg from the accident. I spent two weeks in intensive care and I am happy to report that I made a full recovery minus one kidney.
It was not only difficult on me but my entire family and in particular my mother who had just experienced the death of my brother just a few months earlier. I believe that it was the prayers of loved ones that lead to my miraculous recovery.

There were times in my life when I struggled with alcohol and other adcictions as a result of the great pain of emptiness that I held in my core until I was 31. I literally had a religious experience that helped me to overcome that pain and let go of it. Today I am a Certified Consciousness Coach. I coach individuals, couples and groups to help them achieve their maximum potential in relationships, lifestyles and businesses. I help coach various groups of ex-offenders, and their family members, on everything from successful re-integration into society and family, and in overcoming addiction. I also coach people who are about to go into prison, and their families, in order to help them get through the experience with constructive results.

Other relevant experiences in my life have come from my previous ambitions and businesses pursuits. I could play the guitar and piano and sing sufficiently to write music, lyrics and sing in a rock band that I formed with my brothers. At one point I even accepted a record contract with a small record company in Los Angeles and had the humbling experience of living the life of a starving artist (literally).

Eventually, I went to the University of Colorado and earned a degree in Electrical Engineering. Ever since 1989, when I opened my first Charles Schwab account, and worked at Dean Witter as an assistant to a broker, I have been fascinated with global financial markets.

I dedicated most of my career as an electrical engineer to the pursuit of developing and using live trading of technical market software systems. As a result of my passion for the markets, I have traded in virtually every significant financial market in the world, either directly or indirectly; sometimes with my own money, sometimes with other people's money. By the time I was 27 I had written a book on technical market analysis, and had formulated several strategies that are still a staple method of trading in the financial markets today.

In between all of that I became a Registered Investment Advisor when I was 29 and built my own International Registered Investment Advising Firm. I worked to help raise money for over 25 publicly traded companies. I've served as an officer and director of 2 international publicly traded companies. I've taken 4 companies public, and was the former founding member of an international investment banking firm based in South Africa, where I lived from 2003 to 2008. In my own former public company we had offices in all over the world including China, Mexico, Africa, Denmark, the EU and the USA. I have worked with analysts, brokers, bankers, market makers, investment advisors, and investors from all over the world.

Unfortunately my lack of experience in corporate governance resulted in one company being delisted from the U.S. Stock Markets, and later resulted in the bankruptcy and closure of the company because of regulatory issues. All this happened just as we were about to finalize billions of dollars worth of international business contracts in several countries. I grew the company so rapidly that it spiraled out of my control too quickly and I took too many shortcuts to try to engineer the outcomes. This eventually led to civil and criminal charges against me, and sadly the loss of jobs for people and losses for some investors. As a result, my family and I lost everything while living in a foreign country with no other means to sustain ourselves. Sadly, many of the sustainable, humanitarian business projects that I had launched in South Africa and Mexico were all unable to get off the ground without the critical financing, which was subsequently lost.

I have made and lost fortunes in the stock market and in my related businesses. I have experienced both the dark side of how markets are made, investors hurt, and the positive side where markets benefit businesses and investors. I have felt the joy of high valuations, where people praised me for the fortunes that I made for them, and I have experienced the suffering and pain of my own loss and the loss of others who believed in me and some of whom vilified me.

I have risked my life, and unfortunately placed the lives of my own family at risk in the past, as a result of working with the U.S. Central Intelligence Agency during international financial work. Some of the work I did for the CIA added to my problems in a criminal case, while the rest was my own responsibility. I thought I knew the risks, but there are consequences. The bulk of all that did happen, and to which I was exposed, will remain known only to myself and others directly involved.

Unfortunately, I was indicted, and later plead guilty to, federal securities fraud charges related to insider trading. I spent over 3 years in a U.S. Federal Prison. It was a very heavy cost for my loved ones and myself.

Being in the business of money has been my life. I have seen how money can bring out the worst and the best in people. I have seen people struggle to come to terms with new financial wealth, and I have seen people lose everything, go into debt and even go to prison as a result of money. I have had the hands on technical experience in many aspects financial markets and banking in various countries that few people ever have the chance to see.

When I was indicted on criminal charges in the U.S. in relation to my former business I was living with my family and I had just started to achieve some success in a new business in South Africa after experiencing the devastating loss of my entire public company two years earlier. My daughter was only 7 months old. My criminal indictment forced my family and I to move back to the United States and in the process we lost everything and our entire lives that we built in South Africa. I had to shut down my new business. It was an extraordinarily painful experience to leave a home that we had finally been able to make, where my daughter was born and to leave all of our friends never knowing if we would ever see South Africa again. It was like losing everything in some kind of disaster. My wife and children flew home separately from me because I was going to be arrested upon my arrival. I was the last to pack up the final things from our house to go into an uncertain future not knowing what was going to happen to me or my family. It was surreal and painful.

The indictment itself was very painful as I was vilified by the prosecutors who also incited the former share holders to lash out against me. It was then that I experienced the vindictiveness and the dark sides of the U.S. Justice System of which I was previously unaware. I was advised by my lawyers that I should not say anything to anyone in response because of the ongoing case. So when false information was released about me again and again I said nothing.   There were many procedural mistakes made throughout my entire case which maximized the negative impacts on my family and helped ensure I received the maximum term of imprisonment.   In short I know what it is like to have had your reputation ruined.

Just after I was indicted on criminal charges my wife's mother died from cancer. And that same year my wife was also diagnosed with breast cancer. Thankfully she survived after a double mastectomy, but the experience of all of these horrible things happening at the same time was like being in a nightmare. But we both survived thanks to the grace of God and our training as

Consciousness Coaches.

Eventually I had to surrender myself for what ended up being over 3 years in prison. During that time I had difficult times. There were times when things would happen outside of prison over which I had no control, and about which I could only pray to God, realizing that life would go on. This is not to mention the difficult circumstances, unusual situations, and people that one is exposed to in prison. There were errors in my case and I studied the law and won an appeal and there were further errors in the subsequent proceedings that made life very challenging as I represented myself in the court while in prison. Throughout the in prison time I chose to better myself for the sake of my family rather than be a burden to them.

In U.S. Federal Prison getting any kind of real education is virtually impossible. However, what they are required to have by law is an amazing library of religious and other self development books, audio tapes and videos. In addition they had regular services in all religions. I made it my business to find out if there was any utility for me, in my walk as a Christian, in studying all of these faiths. I found some amazing tools and practices that I have integrated into my Christian walk that have served me well. Some of these I share in this book.

I spent most of my time making a serious study of all the greatest writings of religion, spirituality, philosophy and psychology. In prison I was able to discuss all of these subjects with people from all walks of life and all faiths. That was a unique experience. If I had a question about the interpretation of a Bible verse in Hebrew I could simply walk over to a Rabbi from Israel who was also incarcerated and he could read the exact Hebrew text. If I had a question about the meaning of a verse from the Koran I could ask a number of Muslims that were also in prison and they could read for me from the Arabic. I tried to leave no stone unturned I read all of the great religious works and some of the faiths that I studied closely included the Hindu, Buddhism, Judaism, Christianity, Islam, Native American, Jehovah's Witnesses, Mormon, Nation of Islam, Rastafari, Voodo, Aliens and the sciences of enlightenment, psychology and all relevant saints and mystics. There were doctors, lawyers and specialists in every field in the same prison and I made good use of my access to them as well as the clergy and psychology staff that worked for the prison and volunteers who gave sermons and courses to us in prison.

I also volunteered and participated in several drug and alcohol treatment programs. One of these was an intensive, in-house treatment program that lasted for 9 months, and was similar to a boot camp without the physical exercise. There were intensive one-on-one and group sessions, where I learned a great deal. I took careful notes and this book is the first of many that I will write, based on what I learned from my research, and what I continue to learn.

I practiced physical fitness, prayer and meditation and gave consciousness coaching sessions to other inmates in between work assignments and studies of U.S. law at the prison. All of my studies reinforced my belief in and love of Christ and my appreciation for God and my love, patience and compassion for all people. I prayed that God would guide my insights and studies so that I would not be influenced by wrong thinking and I have complete faith that God honored those requests because as it states in the Bible, "seek and you shall find," and it was God that I was seeking with all of my being. Because I felt this cloak of protection and guidance from God in some cases I did dare to participate in the religious ceremonies of other faiths in order to find utility but all the while in my own heart I was praying to the God represented by Christ.

In many cases I did indeed find great utility in incorporating some of the thoughts and practices from other faiths into my own Christian worship. In particular I found the practices of Zen and meditation that involves challenging my ordinary thinking at all times to be extraordinarily beneficial in my walk as a Christian. And I learned that there exists a great misunderstanding by many Christians about Zen Buddhism and its practices. This misunderstanding breaks my heart because it prevents many Christians from discovering the utilities of Zen that can help us behave as better human beings and enables us to walk more closely on the Way of Christ and overcoming our own selfishness (sin).

Being incarcerated was an experience that I would not want to repeat again, but eventually I came to treat the prison as a monastery and a Zen camp for myself, complete with celibacy and landscaping work that we were required to do. There was also a hand full of other prisoners devout in their faiths that I considered as monks that sought a continual relationship with God in order to cope with their overly harsh and lengthy prison terms and deal with other personal and relationship hardships. Many of these men did indeed find the forgiveness, love, joy and peace of God that gave them life and light that shined even in the darkness of incarceration. It is these people and even some of the devout spiritual prison staff members that helped reveal the presence of God that exists everywhere even within a prison compound.

Eventually I realized that God was not in some far off heaven or some other destination where I had to go to but that God was all around us and inside of us if we just slow down enough to see. God is in every object, every breath of air, every blade of grass, every insect, animal, person and exists in every smile. The presence of God is inescapable, all I had to do was to practice opening myself up to receive it. I experienced that we are all dependant on each other and that the real spiritual journey to connect with the presence of God was an inward path. Trying to make other people and the "outside" world fit into our ideas of how it should be is the cause of endless suffering for many people. True joy can only be experienced by learning to accept and appreciate life for the way that it actually comes to you while you are in the midst of trying to do anything. I am a great believer in being a person of action and taking a stand for other people and to do what Christ calls us to do because of my love for Christ. And I also know that, at best we are only co-creators with God. The freedom of choice that God gave to us all is a great responsibility with which God has empowered us all and as such I believe we must always do our best to do what Christ would do. Even with our best intentions and best efforts we will still fail from time to time. I believe this is because our perfection is a result of the fact that we were not intended to experience a perfect life that is without problems and challenges to overcome. Life is a gift from God even the good and the bad and life is full of mystery even when it least appears to be a gift. God willing, I intend to write a great deal more about these subjects in books that follow.

I was determined to make the best of a very difficult set of circumstances for my own sake and that of my family and friends and I did my best and God took care of the rest. My family and I survived these events and we became stronger in our faith and as people. We made it through these events using some of the same concepts, ideas and methods that I share in this book.

Although I am very much involved in the business world because of my passion and experience in business and my love of people, the attainment of financial wealth is not the most important thing in my life. I'm older and I'm more interested in spending time with my family and friends, and using all that I've learned and my coaching to do something to help other people while I continue to try to better myself. What I'm trying to do now is to share my experiences and ideas with others, through my fiction and non-fiction books, screenplays and music. I am not afraid any more and I have a great deal of faith. I consider myself an activist that is willing to take stand for the greater good of the human race even if that means that I must sometimes call out my own brothers and sisters in Christ and even those people from other faiths about which I have studied.

I am not here to say that everything I think is right and correct. I'm here to participate in whatever capacities I believe best in alignment with what I believe God is asking from me and in some cases I am content to take no action. I am thankful to God for every breath and for these lives that we have all been given.

My love for all people and my compassion for those who are oppressed and particularly those in prison does not always make me very popular in certain circles even in the "Christian" community and I understand and expect that. And I have experienced that my calling to be a conscience of sorts by actively sharing my thoughts and opinions about many subjects from religion, politics, science and economics also invites criticism, which I am prepared to accept and endure.

ABOUT THE AUTHOR

Eric Majors is recognized as an expert in global financial market analysis and currencies, with a Bachelor of Science Degree in Electrical Engineering from the University of Colorado. Majors is best known for activism in global economic reform and social justice. His books include "Financial Markets And Technical Analysis" (2005), "Dot Money" (2014) and "Dot Money The Global Currency Reserve, Questions and Answer." Majors is also a certified Consciousness Coach, for individuals, couples and groups. He is a business advisor, speaker, teacher, and believer in God and Jesus Christ.

From 2010 to 2013, Mr. Majors was incarcerated in a U.S. Federal Prison after pleading guilty to charges stemming from his work with the CIA and Insider Trading. As a result of the case Majors and his family were stripped of everything but each other. While in prison Mr. Majors engaged in a unique and in-depth study of various faiths, science and psychology, in order to find the most beneficial spiritual practices, thought processes and lifestyle. As a result of his vast studies and real world experience Mr. Majors is now able to share his unique perspective on life in order to help others.

For more information about this book and Eric Majors visit: www.EricMajors.com

ABOUT "DEALING WITH LOSS FOR BELIEVERS AND EVERYONE" THE BOOK

Dealing With Loss is a book that is written from the perspective of a Christian who has studied all major religions and psychology. This book is valuable for people of all faiths, and even those who do not believe in God. The author, Eric Majors, knows about suffering and loss, and about how to regain and maintain peace and joy under difficult circumstances. He knows as a result of the extraordinary challenges and difficult experiences he and his family have struggled with.

This book provides a fundamental understanding of the nature of suffering from loss. It details the essential processes to overcome this suffering that have been successfully used by many people throughout the ages that are now being rediscovered by science.

For more information please visit:
www.EricMajors.com

OTHER BOOKS BY THIS AUTHOR:

ABOUT "DOT MONEY" THE BOOK

Dot Money may be the most important book of our time. It has the potential to transform the world and the lives of every individual for the better. This book explores the creation and use of money, global monetary systems, and our preconceived ideas of money. Then it reveals how ordinary people can take control of the money system today, making it work for them as an alternative to just working to make ends meet. Dot Money is more than a book it is a movement.

Dot Money reveals the next step in the evolution of global economics and shows us how to solve the most important problems of our time. This book has the potential to enable us to overcome poverty, and increase the standard of living for every human being regardless of their current resources, education, race, religion, health, geographic location, political or social affiliations.

For more information please visit:
www.DotMoneyBook.com

ABOUT "DOT MONEY, THE GLOBAL CURRENCY RESERVE, QUESTIONS & ANSWERS"

Dot Money is a new and revolutionary kind of global community currency that incorporates the technology of virtual currencies and adds many new features that enable it to be used with or without computers or the internet. The design and purpose of Dot Money is to introduce a new age of economic prosperity and stability throughout the world and solve some of the most important problems facing the world today, including ending poverty. The Global Currency Reserve (GCR) is the international administrator and primary market maker of Dot Money.

The book "Dot Money, The Global Currency Reserve, Questions & Answers" is designed to enable the reader to become familiar with the purposes and functions of Dot Money and the Global Currency Reserve (GCR). This book is designed to be accompanied by the 2014 book "Dot Money" by Eric Majors (www.DotMoneyBook.com). Dot Money may be the most important book of our time.

For more information please visit:
www.DotMoney.Cash
www.GlobalCurrencyReserve.com